OXFORD BIBLE SERIES

General Editors
P. R. Ackroyd and G. N. Stanton

There are many commentaries on individual books of the Bible but the reader who wishes to take a broader view has less choice. This series is intended to meet this need. Each volume embraces a number of biblical books. Four deal thematically with different kinds of material in the Old Testament: narrative, prophecy, poetry/psalmody, wisdom, and law. Three handle different aspects of the New Testament: from the Gospels, Paul and Pauline Christianity, to varieties of New Testament thought. An additional volume looks at the nature of biblical interpretation, covering both Testaments.

Discussion in detail of selected biblical passages provides examples of the ways in which the interpretation of the text makes possible deeper understanding of the wider issues, both theological and historical, with which the Bible is concerned.

OXFORD BIBLE SERIES

General Editors
P. R. Ackroyd and G. N. Stanton

INTRODUCING THE OLD TESTAMENT

R. J. COGGINS

OXFORD UNIVERSITY PRESS

Oxford University Press, Walton Street, Oxford OX2 6DP

Oxford New York Toronto
Delhi Bombay Calcutta Madras Karachi
Kuala Lumpur Singapore Hong Kong Tokyo
Nairobi Dar es Salaam Cape Town
Melbourne Auckland Madrid
and associated companies in
Berlin Ibadan

Oxford is a trade mark of Oxford University Press

Published in the United States by
Oxford University Press Inc., New York

British Library Cataloguing in Publication Data
Coggins, R. J. (Richard James) 1929–
Introducing the Old Testament
1. Bible. O.T. Critical Studies
I. Title
221.6

ISBN 0-19-213255-5

Library of Congress Cataloging in Publication Data
Coggins, R. J., 1929–
Introducing the Old Testament | R. J. Coggins.
(Oxford Bible series)
Includes Bibliographical references.
1. Bible. O.T.—Introductions.   I. Title.   II. Series.
BS1140.2C64 1989   221.6'1—dc20   89-35933
ISBN 0-19-213255-5

7 9 10 8 6

Printed in Great Britain
on acid-free paper by
Biddles Ltd., Guildford and King's Lynn

GENERAL EDITORS' PREFACE

There are many commentaries on individual books of the Bible, but the reader who wishes to take a broader view has less choice. This series is intended to meet this need. Its structure is thematic, with each volume embracing a number of biblical books. It is designed for use with any of the familiar translations of the Bible; quotations are normally from RSV, but the authors of the individual volumes also use other translations or make their own where this helps to bring out the particular meaning of a passage.

To provide general orientation, there are two volumes of a more introductory character: one considers the Old Testament in its cultural and historical context, the other the New Testament, discussing the origins of Christianity. Four volumes deal with different kinds of material in the Old Testament: narrative, prophecy, poetry/psalmody, wisdom and law. Three volumes handle different aspects of the New Testament: the Gospels, Paul and Pauline Christianity, the varieties of New Testament thought. One volume looks at the nature of biblical interpretation, covering both Testaments. This is designed both to draw together some of the many themes touched on in the other volumes, and also to invite the reader to look further at the problems of understanding an ancient literature in the very different cultural context of the present time.

The authors of the individual volumes write for a general readership. Technical terms and Hebrew or Greek words are explained; the latter are used only when essential to the under-standing of the text. The general introductory volumes are designed to stand on their own, providing a framework, but also to serve to raise some of the questions which the remaining volumes examine in closer detail. All the volumes other than the two general ones include discussion of selected biblical passages in greater depth, thus providing examples of the ways in which the interpretation of the text makes possible deeper understanding of the wider issues, both historical and theological, with which the Bible is concerned.

Select bibliographies in each volume point the way to further discussion of the many issues which remain open to fuller exploration.

P.R.A.
G.N.S.

PREFACE

It is a commonplace that we live in a world which is becoming increasingly complex. No longer can there be any serious expectation of a single individual mastering the whole sum of human knowledge, in the way that was envisaged of Renaissance men such as Leonardo da Vinci or Michelangelo. Even within a single realm of intellectual disciplines, specialization becomes more and more essential. No longer do the real experts claim to be 'chemists' or 'biologists', still less 'scientists' in the broad sense; real grasp is limited to a much more narrowly and precisely defined field.

If this explosion of knowledge is most characteristic of the natural sciences, the humanities are not exempt from the same kind of development. We all know of the historian who refuses to answer the simplest question with a 'Not my period', and biblical study has experienced the same tendency toward greater specialization. In the humanities, however, it is often not the increasing range of knowledge that poses the biggest problems; at least as important is the recognition that related disciplines may have something important to tell the student of history or of literature.

It is to a consideration of some of the ways in which a range of scholarly disciplines has been seen as having light to shed upon the Old Testament that this book is largely devoted. After a brief introductory chapter setting out, in as objective a fashion as possible, what the Old Testament consists of, the main body of the book will attempt to outline the way in which a whole variety of expertise has been applied to its study. As we have already seen, no one can claim to be expert, or even competent, in this whole range of different disciplines (and certainly the present author makes no such claim). Nevertheless, it may be possible to offer something of a guide which will enable those undertaking the serious study of the Old Testament to grasp what kind of scholarly skills have been enlisted in that study. In such a way, the Old Testament may be placed in a larger and more meaningful context.

One important warning must, however, be borne in mind throughout. It arises partly from the fact already mentioned, that no individual can hope to achieve competence in all the different relevant disciplines, partly from an understandable wish on the part of religious believers to maintain the authority of the biblical material. The result may be a tendency to select from a cognate discipline only such data as appear to be directly relevant to the Bible, rather than to see the whole context within which such data exist. Thus, in the field of archaeology, it is tempting to concentrate on sites mentioned in the biblical text, with the hope of correlating archaeological and biblical evidence. But such a procedure can be very misleading; the whole archaeological picture may show that individual pieces of evidence can only properly be interpreted in the light of a much broader context. Thus, if we read that the Israelites captured a city, and we discover from archaeological excavations that the site in question was destroyed at an appropriate period, it is natural to correlate the two pieces of evidence. Natural, certainly; but it could also be highly misleading, and a wider study of the archaeological evidence might show other sites, quite unconnected with the Israelites, being destroyed at the same time. Only by looking at the whole range of available evidence can we hope to build up a balanced picture.

Similar caution will be necessary in the use of all the disciplines mentioned, even though, of course, selection is inevitable; this or any other book can offer only a very partial interpretation of the range of evidence available.

It remains to thank Peter Ackroyd and Graham Stanton, the editors of this series, for inviting me to write this book, and for their patience over the delays that have beset it. I should also like to express my gratitude to several generations of students in University Extra-Mural classes, with whom I have tried to explore some of the ideas set out here, for their willingness to bear with me, and to comment on and criticize what I was trying to say. I hope that future students of this kind may find the book of some value to them.

R.J.C.

CONTENTS

I

What is the Old Testament?

What is the Old Testament? It may seem extraordinary that such a question needs to be put. In fact, much controversy has surrounded both the name 'Old Testament' and the contents of the collection so described; and it is clearly important at the very outset to make clear what it is that we are talking about.

Names of the collection

First, then, the name 'Old Testament'. Since this is the name in common usage for the body of writings to be discussed in this book and the companion volumes, its use will be retained here, but it is right to recognize what a question-begging title it is. It is a *Christian* title applied to a body of Israelite or Jewish writings which were then set alongside other specifically Christian writings to which the title 'New Testament' was given. In other words the giving of the name 'Old Testament' to these writings can legitimately be seen as part of a remarkably successful take-over bid by the Christian Church, to claim for itself the heritage of Judaism. Even the very name 'Israel' is apparently claimed on behalf of the Christian Church (Gal. 6: 16).

There is no single Jewish title which can be described as the equivalent to the Christian use of 'Old Testament'. ('Hebrew Bible', sometimes found in books on the subject, including this one, is not a traditional description, but one devised by modern scholars.) For the Jew the Pentateuch, that is, the first five books, is of central importance: these books are collectively described as the Torah, often but somewhat misleadingly translated as 'the Law' (for a fuller discussion, see (in this series) J. Blenkinsopp, *Wisdom and Law in the Old Testament* (OUP, 1983), pp. 74-5). To it are added the collections known as the Prophets (Nebiim) and the Writings (Ketubim). From the initial letters of these Hebrew names (Torah, Nebiim, Ketubim) the word Tenak has been made up as a designation of the sacred Scriptures. Another name sometimes found is Miqra, meaning that which is recited—a useful reminder that in Judaism the holy writings function first and foremost within the context of the solemn assembly of the synagogue, where they are recited according to precisely defined ritual conventions.

Other titles are found within Judaism, but perhaps enough has been said to illustrate at least two points: first, that the naming of this body of writings is, or should be, a matter of considerable delicacy, whereas Christian triumphalism has too often been conspicuous; and secondly, that the context in which these writings have been preserved is as the sacred texts of religious groups. Western tradition during the last two centuries has decreed that such religious texts should be studied and criticized in the same way as any other text, and that tradition is reflected in this volume and its companions. Again, it is well to recognize that this is an area in which offence can easily be caused; there are those within both Judaism and Christianity for whom such scholarly critical study is anathema. Readers of this book may not share that point of view; but it is at least right to recognize that if there were not this tradition of preserving these writings as sacred Scripture, they would not be available for us to study.

Contents

The second basic question concerns the contents of the Old Testament. (That title for the collection will be used henceforth, for ease of reference, despite the reservations that have already been expressed.) That there are divergences of custom here can be observed by looking at the contents of different modern translations. The *New English Bible*, for example, is available in three volumes: Old Testament, Apocrypha, and New Testament; whereas if one looks at the *Jerusalem Bible* most of the books classified under Apocrypha in NEB are included in the Old Testament. To a large extent this difference reflects differing views of the Bible held by different Christian Churches, and is only of present concern in so far as it is important to avoid confusion in what is being discussed.

The overwhelming majority of references in this book to particular Old Testament passages will be to that body of material whose authority as Scripture is accepted within Judaism and by all the Christian Churches. In Judaism, as we have seen, it is divided into three: Law, Prophets, and Writings. These are perhaps best envisaged as concentric circles, with the Law, the most holy writings, at the heart. The 'five-fifths' of the Law, as it is sometimes described (Genesis, Exodus, Leviticus, Numbers, and Deuteronomy), had been accepted as *the* sacred writing long before the beginning of the Common Era, and such groups as the Samaritans, whose split from the Judaism of Jerusalem was taking place in the last centuries BC, share this reverence for the Torah. (For references to dates the forms 'BC' and 'AD' are retained here because of their familiarity. It should be recognized that, as with the description 'Old Testament', this is distinctively Christian terminology. A system of references to the 'Common Era' (CE) and the period 'Before the Common Era' (BCE) may be coming into more general use.)

The second circle consists of the Prophets (Nebiim). Here it is important to bear in mind that this designation includes the books Joshua, Judges, Samuel, and Kings, known as the Former Prophets, as well as Isaiah, Jeremiah, Ezekiel, and the Twelve (the Minor Prophets from Hosea to Malachi) collectively known as the Latter Prophets. This is an important indication of the fact that the traditional concern is with the prophetic scrolls, and not with the prophets as individuals. In Judaism, the Prophets are primarily understood as commentary upon, and elaboration of, the Torah, and in the synagogue readings each appointed portion of the Torah is accompanied by a portion from the Prophets, known as a Haphtarah (= 'dismissal'). Such an understanding of the prophetic material is strikingly different both from the traditional Christian understanding and from the way in which the prophets have been understood in modern study of the Old Testament.

The third circle is known as the Writings (Ketubim), and so imprecise a title implies that here there is greater diversity. In the usual order of the Hebrew Bible the Writings consist of Psalms, Proverbs, Job, the five Megilloth or festal scrolls (Song of Songs, Ruth, Lamentations, Ecclesiastes, Esther, each associated with a particular annual festival), Daniel, Ezra and Nehemiah, and Chronicles. There are plenty of indications of the fact that these writings have been held on a lower level of veneration than the Law and the Prophets: not all Jewish groups have regarded them as Scripture (cf. again the Samaritans); some Jewish communities have added other writings to these here listed (in Ethiopia, for example, the Jewish and Christian communities have at different times regarded as Scripture the book of Enoch and also Jubilees, a kind of commentary on Genesis and part of Exodus); and these are the books whose order and placing could be modified in the Greek and other translations, as is reflected in the Christian Bible. Indeed, two of these books (Esther and Daniel) took significantly different form in their Greek version, through the addition of extra sections.

The reader familiar with the Christian Bible will recognize that the books named are those which constitute its Old Testament, though there they are thirty-nine in number as against the twenty-four of the Hebrew Bible, a difference achieved by counting the Minor Prophets as twelve rather than one, and by dividing Samuel, Kings, Chronicles, and Ezra-Nehemiah. More important than a different system of enumeration is the difference in order. Whereas the Jewish arrangement is best seen as a series of concentric circles, the Christian order can perhaps be best understood in terms of past, present, and future. The material from Genesis to Esther is historical, dealing with Israel's past and the way her God is believed to have guided her destiny. The next section, from Job to the Song of Songs, can be regarded as dealing with the present needs of the community—its worship (Psalms) and its manner of life (the remaining writings). Finally, the Prophets, including Lamentations, regarded as a kind of appendix to Jeremiah, and Daniel, who had been seen as a prophet in Christian eyes at least from the time of the New Testament writings (Matt. 24: 15). For Christians the Old Testament has traditionally been seen as pointing forward to Jesus Christ at either his first or his expected second coming, and the prophets pre-eminently so. The prophets have thus come to be understood as foretellers, pointing forward in ambiguous and cryptic ways (Heb. 1: 1) to events that were to take place long after their own lifetime. In this way the Christian Old Testament ends on an expectant note, looking forward to a fulfilment yet to be realized.

Transmission

If these are the contents of the Hebrew Bible and Christian Old Testament, how have they come down to us? The first, and perhaps most surprising, fact is that the Christian Old (and New) Testament is at one level 'older' than the Hebrew Bible. The great codices of the Greek Bible—those known as Sinaiticus, Vaticanus, and Alexandrinus—date from approximately the fourth century AD; the oldest *complete* text of the Hebrew Bible is not earlier than the tenth century of our era. The standard scholarly edition of the Hebrew Bible in fact uses a manuscript dating from 1008 AD. To state matters thus baldly is in fact to give a misleading impression, and in the next chapter some consideration will be given to the way in which the material has come down to us. For the moment, however, we may simply note that it is prima facie not surprising that scholars have often been tempted to emend the received Hebrew text on the grounds that reliable transmission over so long a period is hardly to be expected, and that the tradition underlying the Greek versions has sometimes been preferred to the Hebrew text.

That is not our immediate concern, however; for the moment we should simply note that the context in which the material was handed down was a religious one. That is to say, not only are the themes of the Old Testament religious ones: God, prayer, worship, and the like; the texts themselves actually became an integral element in the religion of both Jewish and Christian communities. In the twentieth-century West, influenced by Renaissance and Reformation, we may think of the Bible as a text for private reading or study; but in the medieval period, this was much less frequently the case. The Bible was preserved in both Judaism and Christianity as part of its liturgical inheritance. In the synagogue the solemn chanting of the Torah with its appropriate Haphtarahs formed a climax of the service, and the medieval texts that have come down to us are synagogue texts, supplied with the appropriate indications to the cantor for the correct liturgical chant. In an analogous way the

Christian Church preserved and used the biblical material as an integral part of the Mass and the divine Office recited by the clergy.

The study of the Bible

This point, concerning the manner of transmission of the biblical text, has significant implications for the way in which the Old Testament has been understood. In medieval Judaism, there were numerous scholars who studied the text of the Hebrew Bible in detail and wrote extensively upon it; their commentaries are rightly receiving attention once again in Christian circles, just as they have always been much revered in Judaism. But in the Christian community there was nothing really comparable. It was only with the Reformation, and the renewed emphasis on the authority of Scripture, that the actual biblical text, of both testaments, began to be studied with fresh interest and attention to detail.

And here, of course, may be seen a supreme irony. It was the Protestant Reformation which brought greater attention to the Bible and deeper devotion to its authority and inspiration; and yet it was precisely because of this that an attitude of questioning developed. If the Bible was to be the secure foundation upon which human hopes of salvation rested, then it was essential to know exactly what the Bible consisted of—hence the Protestant rejection of those parts of the Bible not attested in the Hebrew tradition. It was also vital to be sure of its precise meaning, so that doctrines could be genuinely biblical. But once the questioning had begun, it proved impossible to limit it within a safe and acceptable area. The Bible was now no longer simply a part of the deposit of faith preserved by the Church; it was part of Europe's intellectual and religious heritage, which, like every other part of that heritage, would come under critical scrutiny. The result was the development of biblical scholarship in the modern sense: already to some extent in the seventeenth century, and in increasing detail from the mid-eighteenth century onwards. Historical, philosophical, and linguistic questions began to be put to the biblical text; new fields of study produced new modes of understanding, until modern biblical study has become, for many, as arcane a mystery as any of the 'number and hardness of the rules called the *Pie*', the intricate medieval custom of ordering the services of the Church and their biblical readings from which the 1549 Book of Common Prayer hoped to rescue the Church of England. The intention of what follows is not to attempt to evaluate one kind of approach over against other, but to show something of the characteristic concerns and emphases which have led to different ways of understanding the Old Testament. It is sometimes maintained that the loss of the old certainties is much to be deplored, in so far as the Bible is no longer treated as an authority in the way it allegedly once was; it is hoped to show that there are also great gains in the rich variety of insights which modern scholarship can bring to it.

In particular, it is of great importance to know what kind of questions can legitimately and profitably be put to the Bible. Traditionally the religious communities have turned to the biblical text to establish *doctrine*—what is to be believed by members of the community. For roughly the last century there have been those who have regarded the Bible as a sure guide to *history* and who have strongly resisted any challenge to the historical accuracy of any part of the text. A similar approach, often called Fundamentalism, insists that the Bible can also provide accurate information on matters of *science*. All of these assumptions have come under attack; it will be important as we look at different ways of understanding the Old Testament to see what questions it is appropriate to expect it to answer. (This important issue is dealt with more fully in the volume of this series devoted to the interpretation of the biblical material: R. Morgan with J. Barton, *Biblical Interpretation* (OUP, 1988).)

2

What does it Mean?

The first question which must be asked of any text written in a foreign language must be: what does it mean? And so the first kind of expertise of which we must take note is that of the linguist and philologist. Here, though there has been a great increase in our knowledge in modern times, there is no question of a newly discovered discipline; the quest for the precise meaning of the Old Testament has gone on as far back as we can trace.

It will be helpful at the outset to isolate two distinct, though related, issues in this quest for meaning. One concerns the text itself: can we rely upon it? Are what we have in front of us the actual words of the original author? Have those been corrupted, either deliberately or accidentally, before they reached their final form? The other question relates to the actual meaning of the individual words: can we be sure that an accurate memory of what each word has meant has been preserved?

Composition

During the course of this chapter it will be necessary to look at these questions separately, but for the moment they should both be kept in mind as we turn our attention in slightly greater detail to what is known of the process by which the Old Testament came to us. It must be acknowledged at the outset that we are ignorant as to the actual circumstances of composition of all the books of the Old Testament. Some have come to be associated with particular famous individuals—the Torah with Moses; the Psalms with

David; Proverbs, Ecclesiastes, and the Song of Songs with Solomon—and some are linked with a particular prophetic figure. But in none of these cases is it clear what the actual process of composition may have been. In the first group, most scholars would say that the link with Moses and the other figures was only made at a much later period; in the second it seems probable that the prophets were in the first instance speakers, and that their words were only written down at a subsequent stage. The implication of this is that the actual literary deposit will always be the earliest form of which we can speak. However much scholarly progress is made, we shall never be certain of recovering the actual words of (say) Amos; the most that we can hope for is an accurate identification of the earliest stages of the written form of the Amos-tradition. (It may properly be remarked here, though it is not strictly relevant to our immediate concern, that questions about the date of particular books of the Old Testament are usually unanswerable, in the sense that it is not normally possible to establish when material spreading over perhaps centuries reached its final forms. At times, too, when answers to the question of date are offered, they can be traps for the unwary. Thus, the Psalms are sometimes spoken of as 'the Hymnbook of the Second Temple', that is, the temple built around 515 BC. This may be an appropriate answer if one is thinking of the Psalms as a collection; it could be quite misleading if used as a date for individual Psalms in the collection.)

Because of the circumstances that have been set out, it is impossible to know when these writings were set down in a form which could be regarded as authoritative by the community. Such a passage as 1 Chronicles 16: 40, written in or around the fourth century BC, speaks of David's action as being 'according to all that is written in the law (*torah*) of the LORD', and this and other references in the books of Chronicles can probably be taken as implying that at least the Torah was by then not only substantially complete but regarded as authoritative.

The Torah is written in Hebrew; indeed one of the criteria later applied within Judaism for which books could be regarded as sacred was that they should have been written in Hebrew. In fact this requirement is not strictly met; a phrase in Genesis (31: 47), a single verse in the Prophets (Jer. 10: 11), and three more extended sections of the Writings (Dan. 2: 4–7: 28; Ezra 4: 8–6: 18; 7: 12–26) are in Aramaic. The point is of some importance in our present concern, for it seems clear that during the last centuries before the Christian era, Aramaic, which was already widely used as the language of diplomacy and trade between nations (2 Kgs. 18: 26), came gradually to replace Hebrew as the language of everyday use, and Hebrew became a learned or 'religious' language. (It has been much discussed whether Jesus of Nazareth is likely to have had knowledge of Hebrew.) By the time that a fresh body of writing in Hebrew emerged, the Mishnah and other products of Rabbinic Judaism in the second century AD and later, there had been significant developments away from the usage of biblical Hebrew, and therefore this later material cannot be used in any automatic way to close gaps in our knowledge of the biblical language. (The same is, of course, true to an even greater extent of Modern Hebrew as used in the state of Israel, a language which is largely an artificial construction.) Though it may be the case that insufficient use has been made of these later developments of the language in the attempt to resolve biblical linguistic puzzles, there would be general agreement that few certain answers can be obtained by that means.

The meaning of the text

We shall return to the first of the two questions with which we began this chapter—the reliability of the text—at a later stage (see p. 18), but for the moment further consideration can be given to this question of meaning. How far can we be sure of the meaning of individual words? It should be recognized at the outset that the problematic area is a limited one; though particular usage may be disputed there is no real doubt as to the meaning of all the more common terms, and many others can clearly be identified by means of the context in which they appear. There remains a residue, usually words which occur only once or twice in the Hebrew Bible, often in poetry, about whose meaning there is real ground for uncertainty. On what principles should such uncertainty be resolved?

Textual criticism

Very broadly speaking, three types of approach have won favour. One is to assume that in cases of difficulty an error has crept into the text, and to emend the text so as to produce a more acceptable form. This is known as conjectural emendation. A second way is to assume that the ancient translations of the Bible, especially that into Greek, which, as we have seen, antedates all surviving Hebrew texts of the complete Old Testament, will have preserved a better understanding of the original meaning. (For the Torah, this second approach does not even need to turn to translations, for the Samaritans have preserved their own Samaritan Pentateuch, which differs in some important details from the Hebrew text of our Old Testament, and is sometimes regarded as preferable.) Thirdly, it may be the case that words otherwise unknown in Hebrew have been preserved in other ancient Semitic languages such as Akkadian (the language of ancient Babylonia) and light may be shed on the meaning of the Hebrew text by recourse to these other languages as well as to other Semitic languages such as Arabic which developed at a later period but may have preserved ancient vocabulary. The first two approaches will most frequently involve some correction of the existing Hebrew text, on the assumption that that form has in some way been corrupted; the third approach characteristically retains the existing text, maintaining that the form is right, but that the actual meaning of the words has been misunderstood.

On some occasions the translation problem arises less from individual difficult words than from the apparent meaninglessness of a whole phrase. There then arises a fourth way of rendering Hebrew into a modern language, though one hesitates to call it a 'method'. This is simply to render the Hebrew words by apparent English equivalents, regardless of whether the resultant English produces an acceptable meaning. Though perhaps characteristic of students in their early struggles with the language it is by no means unknown in more exalted contexts. Thus the AV of Job 19: 20 concludes:

I am escaped with the skin of my teeth.

Such has been the influence of the AV that this expression, usually in the form 'by the skin . . .' has become a proverbial way of describing a narrow escape. But a moment's reflection will show that it is a very odd phrase indeed: teeth do not have 'skin' in any normal sense, and it appears as if the Authorized Version translators were simply forced to rely upon a literal rendering of doubtful meaning.

It is instructive to observe what more recent translations of the Old Testament have done with this verse. RSV illustrates the way in which even a meaningless translation can take on a life of its own; it assumes that the general sense of the verse is the description of a narrow escape, and so follows AV in rendering:

> I have escaped by the skin of my teeth.

No other major modern translation appears to retain this precise rendering, though Good News Bible (GNB), with a note that the Hebrew is obscure, has

> I have barely escaped with my life.

This is in effect a substitute for translation; a paraphrase of what is assumed to be the general sense of a phrase is offered, with no attempt at a precise rendering. This is clearly never wholly satisfactory, but on occasion it may be all that is possible.

On what principles, then, should the translation of this verse proceed? Before detailed examination is given to any one difficulty it will always be a wise precaution to look at the larger context, to see whether a general sense is demanded. Here, unfortunately, there is no agreement. Some scholars have supposed that the sense is that of a narrow escape: the suffering Job, wretched though his condition is, is at least aware that he is still alive and can look to some kind of future. Others have argued that it is only the verb translated 'escape' in this verse which suggests that theme, and that the whole emphasis of the passage is on Job's distress at the continuing misery brought about by his afflictions. In the absence of any clear contextual guidance, commentators and translators have been forced back on one or other of the three methods already outlined: conjectural emendation, resort to the ancient versions, or supplying a meaning for the Hebrew based on other languages. Each of these approaches has been employed for this verse.

It is first of all necessary to offer a literal translation of the whole verse, for the first half is also not free from difficulties. The Revised Version (RV), always a very literal translation, rendered:

> My bone cleaveth to my skin and to my flesh,
> And I am escaped with the skin of my teeth.

Those scholars who have felt that corruption has affected this text in a way which requires emendation note the repetition of the word 'skin' in each half of the verse, recognize that such repetition is not a usual feature of Hebrew poetry, and question the appropriateness in the context of any reference to the flesh. On this occasion, then, no alteration of words is involved, but by deleting the reference to the flesh NEB translates the first line:

> My bones stick out through my skin.

'Bones' for the original 'bone' is not accompanied by a footnote and it may be accepted as legitimate that the singular 'bone' is a kind of collective; 'stick out through' has the note '*lit.* cling to', though one might have thought that the two expressions were almost opposite in meaning; an additional note says '*Heb. adds* and my flesh', which is deleted without explanation.

The second approach was to turn to the ancient versions. The Greek translation, usually referred to as the Septuagint (LXX), translated literally, runs:

> In my skin the flesh rots,
> My bones are held in teeth.

The Jerusalem Bible, originating from a Catholic context in which recourse to the Greek and Latin versions has been more usual than in Protestant circles, follows that practice here in its rendering:

> Beneath my skin, my flesh begins to rot,
> and my bones stick out like teeth.

Here, obviously the sense of 'escape' has been completely eliminated and the context is taken to be a continuation of Job's cry of anguish. In such a context the translation makes good sense; the difficulty inevitably lies in the uncertainty whether LXX was rendering the original Hebrew accurately or was itself trying to make the best of a text which was no longer understood at the time of the translation.

To illustrate our third approach we may turn again to the NEB, in which the second line is rendered:

> and I gnaw my under-lip with my teeth.

For this no footnote is provided, for it is alleged that the words normally translated 'escape' and 'skin' are not in fact those words at all, but homonymous forms (i.e. words written in the same way but with a different meaning). The first is claimed as a word found in Akkadian and Arabic with the sense of 'rub' or 'gnaw', the second is an Arabic word for the 'bottom palate'.

Detailed consideration has been given to one verse to explain discrepancies in translation which must catch the attention of any alert reader, and to illustrate the principles underlying different ways of resolving these discrepancies. It will perhaps be clear that no single principle is likely to win universal support, and in poetic books such as Job examples of such discrepancies could be multiplied.

There is one other characteristic feature of textual criticism which is not represented in this example: the proposal that a change is needed in the actual wording of the text as it has come down to us. Here we may take an example from Isaiah 21. Verses 6–12 of that chapter picture the prophet as a watchman, warning his fellow-citizens of impending danger. Verse 7, literally translated, begins, 'And he cried as a lion, "O Lord, I stand continually upon the watchtower" ', and this is the translation of RV. But there is no obvious reason for a reference to a lion, and commentators had long proposed an emendation, suggesting that the word *aryeh*, lion, should be replaced with some form of the verb *raah*, to see. This suggested change was dramatically supported by the discovery of the Isaiah manuscript among the Dead Sea Scrolls, which has the word *haroeh*, 'the one who sees', and no mention of a lion! Hence we arrive at the RSV translation, 'Then he who saw cried . . .'. What had previously been a purely speculative emendation thus received dramatic support. In this field certainty is never possible; it is obviously conceivable that the scribe who composed the scroll made the change because he too was puzzled by a reference to a lion! But most would agree that the text as amended is likely to be closer to the original. The possibility of a copyist's error between the time of the Dead Sea Scrolls (*c.* 2nd cent. BC) and the time of our final text is certainly not to be excluded.

When the text had reached its final form the scribes went to immense care to avoid error by counting the number of words and letters in each book, and these details are recorded in the 'official' Hebrew text as it has been handed down. Perhaps ancient scribal standards were higher than those often found today, when a word processor may induce a false sense of security!

Two concluding notes may be in order in this area. First, we have already noted that this whole question of establishing a precise meaning has been a continuing concern in Judaism and Christianity down the ages. Characteristically the often very shrewd insights of the medieval Jewish commentators have been neglected by modern students; there is currently a welcome tendency to look anew at these works to learn from them.

Secondly, the third of the three approaches sketched out above, involving comparison between Hebrew and other Semitic languages, is an area of great dispute. There can be no doubt that some modern linguistic discoveries, particularly the decipherment of a new dialect or language, have been treated as a kind of magical charm, a new key able to open all the previously locked secrets of the Old Testament. The extensive discoveries at Ras Shamra (the ancient Ugarit), between the two world wars, have led some scholars to suppose that problems in the Hebrew Bible can all be solved by attention to this or that usage in Ugaritic. The more recent discoveries at Tell Mardik (ancient Ebla) have produced a rash of comparable suggestions. (For the archaeological significance of these discoveries, see below, ch. 4.) Others have put forward arguments purporting to show that Arabic, or Akkadian, or other languages, hold the key.

Too often such proposals reflect the fallacious belief that the grass in the neighbour's garden is greener. Uncertainties as to the meaning of Ugaritic texts; doubts as to the dates of particular Arabic usage; questions as to the real formal equivalence between words in different languages—problems of this kind must always be borne in mind when a 'comparative' solution to any uncertainty within the Hebrew Bible is proposed.

It is nevertheless true that on rare occasions light on the meaning of the text may come from quite unexpected sources. In the book of Proverbs there is a sudden change in literary form at 22: 17. The preceding material is of the kind which we might call 'proverbs' today; what follows is instruction. Early in this century an Egyptian text was discovered to be substantially identical in form with the section which begins at this point, and from that link the meaning of a word previously unknown was established. Proverbs 22: 20 in the RV reads:

> Have not I written unto thee excellent things?—

with the meaning of the word translated 'excellent' being unknown. In the RSV we find (and other modern translations are equivalent):

> Have I not written for you thirty sayings?

The reference, it is now clear, is to the list of instructions which follow, both in Proverbs and in the Egyptian Instruction of Amen-em-ope, upon which Proverbs is based. Even in so small a detail as this, it is striking how an unexpected new light can be shed on our understanding of the Old Testament text. But such precise correlation is very rare indeed.

Hebrew idiom

Meaning does not reside only in individual words. It would be possible to 'translate' from French or German into English by looking up each individual word in a dictionary, and to come up with a rendering which was either nonsense or a complete misrepresentation of the sense of the original. The idiom of each language must also be taken into account. The same is true with Hebrew. It is clearly not appropriate in a book of this kind to discuss Hebrew idiom in any detail, but two examples may be given of the way in which awareness of appropriate idiom is essential for a proper understanding of the Old Testament.

It is not always easy to distinguish poetry from rhythmic prose in the Hebrew Bible, but the former in particular may be characterized by the usage known as parallelism. First recognized among moderns, it is said, by the eighteenth-century bishop Robert Lowth, this is the device whereby the second line is simply a variation on the first, either through repetition of the same thought in synonymous terms:

> The heavens/are telling/the glory of God;
> and the firmanent/proclaims/his handiwork;   (Ps. 19: 1)

or by the setting out of antitheses in the two lines:

> They/will collapse/and fall
> but we/shall rise/and stand upright.   (Ps. 20: 8)

The New Testament provides one familiar example which suggests that this device was not universally recognized at that time. In Zechariah 9: 9 we find an example of parallelism of a slightly more elaborate type:

> Lo, your king comes to you:
> triumphant/and victorious is he
> humble/and riding on an ass,
> on a colt the foal of an ass.

(It should be noted that the word translated 'humble' is disputed, and that two different Hebrew words are translated 'ass' by RSV.) In the Gospel of Matthew this passage is quoted (21: 5), but the literary convention seems not to be recognized, and the accompanying story (vv. 2, 7) makes mention of *two* animals, with Jesus somewhat incongruously made to ride both.

The second characteristic feature of Hebrew usage which needs to be understood is given the technical name 'merismus'. It describes the custom of using paired opposites to describe a totality. Sometimes the point is obvious. We should understand:

> both low and high,
> rich and poor together   (Ps. 49: 2)

to imply everyone, even if the point had not been made explicitly in the previous verse:

Give ear, all inhabitants of the world.

On other occasions this literary form (which is not confined to poetry) may, if its presence be established, alter the meaning of a passage very significantly. Thus, in the second creation story in Genesis, the tree in the middle of the garden is described as 'the tree of the knowledge of good and evil' (Gen. 2: 17). Does 'good and evil' here imply moral discernment, the ability to distinguish good from evil? Or is this a merismus, implying knowledge of everything? Most who have written on the passage have preferred the first alternative, but it is at least arguable that this reads into the passage something that is not there. The attentive reader will soon discover that this particular literary usage is a specially characteristic feature of the Old Testament.

The reliability of the text

Many other distinctive elements in Hebrew usage could be quoted, but it is necessary now to revert to the first of the two questions with which we began this chapter: can we rely upon the text in the form in which it has come down to us as substantially in accord with the intentions of its original author? We have already noted that it would be foreign to the character of copyists, ancient or modern, to suppose that any literary work would be passed down for many generations totally free from error, but there is clearly a substantial difference between minor copyists' errors and a basic corruption which involves the loss of the original meaning. (Few modern books are totally free of misprints; but it is mercifully very rare for these to be so serious as to raise doubts about the sense of what is written.)

We have seen already that the earliest complete manuscripts of the Hebrew Bible are not earlier than the tenth century of our era, and this implies a gap of more than a millennium between the original 'autograph' and the earliest copy to which we have access. It was the awareness of this lengthy gap that led many scholars of an earlier generation to put forward extensive proposals for emending the received Hebrew text—the first of the three methods of overcoming difficulties of meaning which we noted in the previous section. A glance at a critical commentary, especially on a poetic text, of the period between roughly 1900 and 1939 will provide ample illustration of this custom.

More recently, however, this willingness to emend the text has been much less in evidence; and it is instructive to enquire why this should be so. The first, and perhaps most important, reason is the discovery of the Dead Sea Scrolls from Qumran. The first of these scrolls were discovered in 1947, and they became available for scholarly investigation within a very short time. In the 1950s there were scholars of repute who remained convinced that the scrolls were medieval, but it is now all but universally agreed that they date back to the last centuries before the Christian era. Among these scrolls biblical texts have been prominent—two of the very first discoveries were of the book of Isaiah, one complete, the other a part—and all modern translations of the Old Testament have taken into consideration the evidence of the scrolls.

To a remarkable extent the evidence of the scrolls has confirmed the reliability of the textual tradition enshrined in our Old Testament over a period of more than 1,000 years. The RSV, one of the first modern translations to include the scrolls in its assessment of the evidence, made thirteen changes in its rendering of the book of Isaiah on the basis of the Qumran evidence. Nearly all of these concern the meaning of a single word, such as that at 21: 8 which we noted earlier. Now this is not to claim that all difficulties in the meaning of the book of Isaiah have been resolved, and clearly an officially approved translation will err on the side of caution and not engage in excessive speculation. Nevertheless it would have seemed incredible to many scholars before the discovery of the scrolls, if they had been told that evidence 1,000 years earlier than that with which they were accustomed to work would uphold the existing text to so great an extent.

It is of course clear that the Qumran discoveries raise a much wider range of issues, and it is perhaps not surprising that a whole mini-industry, with specialist journals and the like, should have grown up around Qumran studies. It has already been seen that as far as the detailed transmission of the text is concerned, the Qumran evidence by and large points in a conservative direction, that is to say, the actual transmission was a more accurate process than had previously been envisaged by some scholars. In other respects, however, the Qumran evidence is by no means so unambiguous, and to appreciate this we shall need to consider what is known of the way in which the present text arose.

We have seen already that our earliest surviving Hebrew Bibles date from around the eleventh century AD. The text of the Hebrew Bible which they incorporate is known as the Massoretic Text (MT); the name comes from the detailed marginal notes which had accumulated and served as a means of ensuring the accurate transmission of the text. The word *massora* means 'tradition', and those who preserved and handed down the traditions accurately were the *Massoretes*. (There is still no agreement whether the more appropriate English rendering of this group of words should be with one 's' or two.)

Varying textual traditions

We have indicated already that these traditionists preserved the material they received with considerable accuracy; but they also selected among a diversity of possible texts. Unfortunately no other biblical scroll of the quality of the complete Isaiah scroll has survived from Qumran, but there is sufficient evidence to show that in some cases, for example the books of Samuel, the Qumran text embodied a tradition significantly different in numerous details from that which came to be enshrined in the Massoretic Text. These differences are not simply a matter of scribal corrections or errors; rather, they imply that in some respects a different text was being handed down. (It is easy for modern readers to forget the extent to which each book in the ancient world was a new and distinct product. In this book, all copies produced by the same mechanical process will be identical, and a reference to, say, p. 20 in one copy will be equally appropriate for every other copy. Before the invention of printing that was simply not so, and the elaborate devices of the Massoretes to ensure that a complete and accurate text was preserved are thus better understood.)

If then we revert to the question with which we began this section—are what we have in front of us the actual words of the original author?—the honest answer has to be that we have no means of being sure. It might seem natural to suppose that the further back we trace the text of a given book, and thus penetrate nearer to the time of its original composition, the less complex the textual history would become. In fact textual critics regularly discover that the reverse is the case; the history they can trace proves to be a history of standardization of an earlier form which was more complex than what has finally come down to us. One more example will illustrate the point. It has long been noted that the book of Jeremiah is very different in its Greek (LXX) form from that with which we are confronted in our Old Testament. The LXX is substantially shorter and contains some sections in a different order. Generations of textual critics have worked on the principle that one of these forms must be significantly closer to 'the original', so that either the LXX represents an abbreviation of the earlier Hebrew, or the Hebrew form underlying our present LXX has been elaborated to form the present Hebrew text. In fact, the more evidence is accumulated, the more it appears that there were at least these two forms of the Jeremiah tradition going back as far as we can trace, with no clear indication that priority must be accorded to one rather than the other. In this particular instance the Qumran evidence is much less substantial than that available for Isaiah, but the Jeremiah fragments that have been discovered point to a Hebrew text much closer to the LXX than to the Hebrew text which has come down to us.

The importance of this diversity must be taken into account, but it should not be exaggerated. Like the textual problems looked at earlier in this chapter, these difficulties as to the precise form of particular books affect only the details of transmission. The great majority of the Jeremiah material is common to both traditions, and, while we should guard against rash generalizations on the nature of the transmission of prophetic words, we need not suppose that there is fundamental uncertainty as to the contents of the tradition. And what is true of Jeremiah is true to an even greater extent elsewhere in the Old Testament, where differences between different textual forms are much less marked. Textual criticism is a discipline whose necessity will continue, and one which must always be taken into account, not least when we want to understand more fully the history of interpretation of a biblical book; its contribution is nevertheless a limited and preliminary one.

3

Did it all Happen?

The first words of the Bible, in practically every translation, are 'In the beginning'. From the very outset, that is to say, the biblical record is presented to us as a series of events that took place at a definite time in history, a history, moreover, whose beginnings could be traced. An earlier generation of biblical scholars expended great energy and learning in working out the date of every event from creation onward, and many editions of the Authorized Version included the dating system worked out in the seventeenth century by Archbishop Ussher of Armagh, according to which creation took place in the year 4004 BC.

Such detailed attention to historical questions might scarcely appear to need justification, for it seems to be amply explained by the concern of the biblical books themselves. Leviticus and Deuteronomy do not advance the historical record in any significant way, but they are placed in particular historical contexts; and all the remaining books of the Pentateuch and the Former Prophets (what we in English often call the Historical Books: Joshua, Judges, Samuel, Kings) have an overwhelmingly historical concern. In the English Bible, which as we have already seen (above, ch. 1) differs in its order from the Hebrew Bible, more historical books are added: 1 and 2 Chronicles, Ezra, Nehemiah, and Esther. Even in the prophetic collections historical allusions abound. It is scarcely to be wondered at that a great deal of modern Old Testament study has taken a predominantly historical form. In particular this has shown itself in two ways which will be our especial concern in this chapter. The first is the basic historical question: did it all happen? The second is the necessity to observe the fact that many modern introductions to the Old Testament have placed virtually the whole of the material within a historical context. We shall need to give some consideration to both the strengths and limitations of that approach.

One of the areas of the explosion of knowledge to which reference was made in the introduction has been the history of the ancient world. Until approximately the beginning of the nineteenth century the Old Testament was treated as a world in isolation, not set in any particular historical context. In 1829 H. H. Milman, later to become dean of St Paul's, published his *History of the Jews*, which caused great offence by treating its subject like any other people of the ancient world; Abraham, for example, was likened to a powerful Oriental sheikh. (There is a nice irony in the fact that conservative churchmen were the leading objectors to Milman; in more recent times one of the main tenets of conservative scholarship has been its reliance on similarities between Israel and its ancient Near Eastern neighbours as a means of establishing the antiquity of customs referred to in the Old Testament).

Objections of the kind raised against Milman could not, however, be long sustained, and to an increasing extent scholars have felt able to place Israel securely within the context of the history of the ancient Near East. That this is true from the eighth century BC until the capture of Jerusalem in 597 is beyond serious doubt; the biblical record, found particularly in 2 Kings, but also in the prophetic books, especially Isaiah and Jeremiah, can be correlated, often in considerable detail, with the annals of the Assyrians and Babylonians, now to be found in the British Museum, London. The biblical texts raise theological and literary as well as historical issues in their interpretation, and there are, of course, problems in the exact correlation of their historical statements with the Assyrian and Babylonian records. But these problems are precisely that, *historical* problems, whose resolution will involve methods of historical study that are appropriate for many different periods and peoples.

Israel and Assyria

As to the period when such correlations first begin to be possible there is more dispute. The first Israelite character to be mentioned

in an extra-biblical text is Ahab, king of the northern kingdom of
Israel in 853, when he played a leading part in the coalition which
joined together to resist the advance of the Assyrian king
Shalmaneser III in the battle of Qarqar. Though the Assyrians
claimed victory, their advance was halted and the coalition of local
states may have been effective—more so, at least, than was Jehu,
another king of Israel, some ten years later, who is represented on
the 'Black Obelisk' of Shalmaneser (also in the British Museum)
doing obeisance to the Assyrian king.

These two references certainly add interest to the Old Testament
accounts of these kings, but they also pose problems for our
understanding of the Old Testament as history. One major
difficulty is that in the Old Testament the Assyrians are not
mentioned in connection with either Ahab or Jehu, and a further
problem arises in the Assyrian reference to Ahab in that it pictures
him in alliance with the king of Damascus, whereas the Old
Testament has Ahab in continuous warfare against the Aramean
kingdom of Damascus. Obviously alliances could develop and
enmities be resolved, but at the very least we are warned that the
account we have is a partial one, and that the story of the northern
kingdom in particular is often shaped by theological bias: for the
editors of the books of Kings the very fact of the existence of a
northern kingdom, no longer subject to the chosen line of David,
was itself an offence, a rebellion against God's chosen ruler (1 Kgs.
12: 19).

The story of David

The mention of David raises a further difficulty. The period from
Saul to Solomon is described in greater detail than perhaps any
other period of the people's history—more than sixty chapters of
the biblical text to cover three generations—and nearly all would
agree that there are enshrined here genuine historical traditions.
But it is also to be borne in mind that the picture of David in
particular is highly idealized, that the achievement of Saul appears
to be deliberately played down in order to glorify David, and that
throughout 1 and 2 Samuel legendary and folkloristic traits (giant-
killing; the rejection of seven contenders and the choice of the

eighth and youngest) are found alongside details which suggest a much more precise degree of historicity.

It is instructive to note that here no precise chronology is available, as it is within a decade or less for the whole period of the divided monarchy. David and Solomon, by contrast, are each credited with a reign of the conventional complete generation of forty years (2 Sam. 5: 4; 1 Kgs. 2: 11; 11: 42), while the tradition regarding Saul's reign has become hopelessly obscured. A literal translation of 1 Samuel 13: 1, which appears to give details of his age and length of reign, would be: 'Saul was one year old when he began to reign and he reigned two years over Israel'. (It is instructive, in view of our discussion of translation problems in the previous section, to note how different modern versions have handled this verse. Jerusalem Bible omits the verse entirely; RSV replaces the numbers with '. . .'; NEB has 'Saul was 50 years old . . . and he reigned for 22 years'.) In the following account of Saul's reign it would not be difficult to construct a scenario which understood Saul as the legitimate ruler, struggling desperately to hold his nascent kingdom together as a unity and widely supported by his subjects (1 Sam. 23: 6–14 is revealing here), whereas David was the unscrupulous rebel, killing all who might inform against him and prepared to ally himself with the Philistines, Saul's and Israel's bitter enemy, when it suited his own ends (1 Sam. 29). Needless to say, this is not the reading offered by the biblical account, for which David's rise was part of God's plan.

One other problem concerning the historicity of the biblical account of this period may be mentioned. One of the most vivid of all narrative sections in the whole Bible is found in 2 Samuel 9–20, 1 Kings 1–2. It is sometimes called the 'succession narrative' or 'court history' because of the gripping account which it gives of the various intrigues which took place at the royal court as different members of David's family staked their claim to the right of succession. Many scholars have held this material in very high regard as historical writing—indeed it has been described as 'The Beginnings of Historical Writing in Ancient Israel' (the title of a well-known study by G. von Rad), and regarded as a reliable source of first-hand information, composed by one of the participants. It is certainly an absorbing story, but it is much more doubtful whether the narrator's skill should be understood as implying historical accuracy. The account of David's dealings with Uriah and Bathsheba (2 Sam. 11) or the story of the rape of the unhappy Tamar, for example (2 Sam. 13: 1–19), must surely owe a great deal to the narrator's imaginative art. Not surprisingly, therefore, recent writers have been much more cautious in treating the succession narrative as a reliable historical account; greater attention is paid nowadays to its remarkable literary character.

Yet it would be wrong to suppose that the accounts of the reign of David and Solomon contain no historical information. Such details as the sober lists of court officials (2 Sam. 8: 16–18; 20: 23–6) make it virtually certain that we are here in a situation where a fully fledged royal administration was being established. So too with some of the details of Solomon's temple (1 Kgs. 6–7), which appear to have made use of early records.

Part of our difficulty in evaluating the accounts of this period historically arises from the fact that neither David nor Solomon is mentioned in ancient sources other than the Old Testament itself, though it would be no great surprise if such a reference did one day emerge. Some would feel that the reason for this silence in the ancient sources was that in their period no great power was eager and able to impose its own authority on Palestine: Egypt was in political decline, Assyria was fully occupied on its other frontiers. Others would take the view that the silence of the sources was due rather to the fact that the achievement and importance of both David and Solomon have been greatly exaggerated by the Old Testament; their importance was purely local and Israel was never remotely one of the great powers. It will be seen that opportunities for differences of view among historians are here considerable, with the issue often turning on dispute as to where the onus of proof should lie: does the silence of other sources make the biblical account automatically suspect, or should it be accepted until it is clearly disproved?

The Persian period

The historical difficulties become even greater when we consider earlier periods, but before doing that it may first be worth while to note that the later Old Testament period also poses problems, though of a rather different kind. The Persian Empire, which controlled Palestine for two centuries (*c.* 530–330), has left nothing comparable with the Assyrian and Babylonian records, and the Old Testament itself is much less rich in the type of narrative material which provides the traditional basis for historical reconstruction. There were no longer nation-states, Israel and Judah; instead the people were part of a larger empire covering the whole area of the Levant: Babylon, then Persia, and then the various Hellenistic powers which followed Alexander the Great. On the one hand this meant that it was inherently less likely that there would be references to Israelites in the records of other states; and on the other hand it had the consequence that the Israelites themselves looked back to earlier times as their own great days. This later period thus contains almost nothing which can be compared to the record of the books of Kings. The books of Ezra and Nehemiah pose considerable problems of interpretation, but do shed some light on a limited period, probably in the fifth century BC. Otherwise it is only with the second century, and the books of Maccabees, in the Apocrypha, that we once again encounter detailed historio-graphical material. And even here it is striking that the two books of Maccabees (which are parallel rather than successive accounts) should differ so markedly in their assessment of the same events.

The beginnings of history

'Did it all happen?' is the title of this chapter, and we have seen that for the monarchical period it is possible to give an affirmative answer, at least as far as the major events on a national scale are concerned. Even there we need to recognize the selective nature of our sources, so that this history is very much a history of kings rather than of a people as a whole and much detail remains uncertain. What about earlier times? Here the difficulties are much greater. There are very few relevant allusions in the records of other states, and it must in any case be clear that the Old Testament material itself is of a very different order from that dealing with the monarchical age.

The pre-monarchical material may quite naturally be divided into four: the time from Adam to Abraham described in Genesis 1–

11; the patriarchs, especially Abraham and Jacob (Gen. 12–36); the period away from Palestine, first in Egypt and then in the wilderness (Gen. 37–Deut.); and the time of settlement in Palestine and the establishment of rule by judges (Josh.–Judg.). It will be convenient to discuss these four periods briefly in reverse order.

The 'judges period'

With regard to the traditions embodied in Joshua and Judges there is little room for doubt that historical elements are incorporated within them. Though there is no external testimony that can be used to support any particular detail, the overall picture given in these books accords very well with the outline that is available. Egyptian control over Palestine had broken down, and there was much conflict in the region, with local rulers and the inhabitants of the desert fringes each trying to establish themselves in power. The former can be typified by Sisera, who is portrayed in Judges 4–5; the latter by the Midianites, whose defeat by Gideon is the basic theme of Judges 6–8.

What in all this is the correct understanding of Israel itself? The biblical account, accepted without question by the vast majority of scholars until recent years, has it that Israel came into Palestine after a long period of a wandering existence in the wilderness or desert area south and east of the cultivated land. That is to say, Israel could in many ways be compared with Midianites, Moabites, or Edomites, since all of them were held to be groups of semi-nomadic origin striving for a settled place in which to establish themselves. The lure of the 'land flowing with milk and honey' would have been powerful for those whose lives were spent on the very margins of settled existence.

Such a view has recently been challenged. The 'common-sense' assumption (which may well be rooted in the values of Western society) that those who live in a subsistence economy on the edge of the desert will eagerly transfer to more fertile territory at the first opportunity has in fact very little solid evidence to support it. Rather, it has been suggested, we should envisage the origins of Israel along the lines of a 'peasants' revolt', an internal uprising. Its specific cause may have been the arrival of some who had successfully escaped from Egyptian power, and told a story of the power of their God as a deliverer, but the main body of those who subsequently became known as Israel were already among the oppressed lower classes of Canaanite society.

This example of a drastic revision of the accepted historical outline is currently a matter of much scholarly debate. (It will be considered again when we look at the perception of Israel as a society in ch. 5). For our purpose it is instructive for two reasons. First, it shows how even the most basic and hitherto unchallenged assumptions will properly come under scrutiny. Secondly, it serves to remind us of the extent to which the larger historical framework within which we place the detailed accounts in the Old Testament is a modern construct, based on an idealized account offered in the Old Testament, as later generations interpreted their past experiences as a way to the understanding of their present situation. The Bible tells us of Israelite victories over or defeats by individual enemies; but the editors of the books of Joshua and Judges use this material as illustrative of God's power to save or punish his people. It has been a matter of modern reconstruction to place these events in a proposed overall historical setting.

For the time of settlement in Palestine, then, we may conclude that a good deal of ancient and probably reliable tradition has come down to us, and that the material of Joshua and Judges is 'historical' in that sense. (On the historicity of individual details and indeed whole episodes, there will of course always be room for differing opinions.) Much more difficult is the claim for a historical basis if by that is meant an overview of the development of a particular nation-state, with precise dates, the details of relations with neighbouring peoples, and the like. At the very simplest level it is instructive to bear in mind that, during the period of Joshua and Judges, Egypt claimed control of Palestine; but there is no reference to contemporary Egyptian power in either of those books.

The Exodus

When we turn to the earlier period, references to Egyptian power abound, for the central event in Israel's tradition of her own history

was the Exodus from Egypt. Israel's understanding of her God as
primarily the deliverer from Egyptian servitude is found all through
the Old Testament from the Ten Commandments onwards: 'I am
the LORD your God, who brought you out of the land of Egypt, out
of the house of bondage' (Exod. 20: 2). That some of the ancestors
of later Israel had been in Egypt need not be doubted, and, as we
have seen, even those who propose a radically new understanding of
Israel's origins accept that the catalyst for the uprising will have
been the arrival of those who spoke of the power of their God in
delivering them from Egyptian control. But problems arise when
the attempt is made to relate the Egypt and wilderness traditions to
a specific set of historical circumstances. We have noted that the
traditions in Joshua and Judges were told not so much as historical
accounts as we should understand the term, but rather as
illustrative, perhaps in the context of religious festivals, of God's
control of events and the way in which he dealt with his people.
With the stories of the departure from Egypt this element of divine
intervention is overwhelming. It seems clear that the account
of God's saving act in the Exodus was handed down in some form
of cultic ceremony, probably to be associated with the Feast of
Passover; and it is indeed a matter for debate whether an existing cultic celebration gave rise to the actual story of the Exodus,
or whether a historical event was the focus of a later cultic
celebration.

Without becoming involved in that particular discussion (which
seems unlikely to be resolved for lack of generally agreed criteria)
we can obtain some idea of possible liturgical usage by looking at
two individual texts. In Psalm 114, the deliverance from Egypt and
the crossing of the Jordan have become inextricably bound together
as if they were alternative versions of one event:

> The sea looked and fled,
>   Jordan turned back.   (Ps. 114: 3)

Even more remarkably, in Isaiah 51: 9–11 the deliverance from
Egypt is woven into an account of creation:

> Was it not thou that didst cut Rahab in pieces,
>   that didst pierce the dragon?

> Was it not thou that didst dry up the sea,
>   the waters of the great deep;
> that didst make the depths of the sea a way
>   for the redeemed to pass over?

Here creation is pictured in terms of struggle against a chaos-monster, named Rahab, or as drying up the waters of the primordial sea; and into that picture is introduced, as if it were all part of the one display of divine power, the divine guidance at the Exodus. Even in the book of Exodus itself it is not difficult to discern differing layers of tradition. In Exodus 14: 21 f., for example, there are two quite different pictures of the deliverance at the sea. In one 'the LORD drove the sea back by a strong east wind all night, and made the sea dry land'; in the other 'the people of Israel went into the midst of the sea on dry ground, the waters being a wall to them on their right and on their left'.

From all this it will become apparent that the usual questions concerning historicity can scarcely be raised here with any likelihood of satisfactory answers. When did all this happen? Who was the Egyptian Pharaoh at the time? Where did the escape take place? These three questions are perhaps the most obvious historical issues; and the character of the data available makes answers to them unattainable. (That is not to say, of course, that the questions stop being asked, or that answers are not proposed; advocates of both a fifteenth- and a thirteenth-century date for the Exodus are still found, and until it proves possible to place the events within the right century, greater precision in historical matters clearly cannot be expected. There are indeed scholars who would maintain that the divergences can only be resolved by supposing that *two* separate departures from Egypt by different groups have been telescoped into one; but such an approach may raise as many problems as it solves.)

One other point with regard to this period should be noted. Much of the material in the books Exodus–Deuteronomy is given over to an account of the laws said to have been revealed through Moses on Mount Sinai. Careful reading of these chapters reveals their remarkably heterogeneous character. In Exodus 21–31, for example, we pass from laws suitable for a community in the earliest stages of its establishment on a settled basis to detailed provisions for the religious rites of priesthood and temple. Such laws are impossible to date, but it seems certain that they reflect changing circumstances in the later development of the community, and that they are attributed to the great lawgiver Moses as a mark of their peculiar authority.

The patriarchs

Moses is credited with a lifespan of 120 years (Deut. 34: 7)—an improbably long but perhaps not a totally incredible age. When we go back one further stage, to the patriarchs, one very obvious shift away from historical credibility is the fact that Abraham, Isaac, and Jacob are credited with even greater lifespans (Gen. 25: 7; 35: 18; 47: 28). It might seem as if this were no more than an example of a widespread tendency to idealize generations long ago, but in a historical consideration it is of some importance. This is not simply because it casts doubt in a general way on the historicity of the material—there is no evidence to support any suggestion that human expectation of life was once significantly greater than it is now—but also because it raises a fundamental ambiguity in the concept of a 'patriarchal age'.

   In the stories in Genesis it is clear that Abraham, Isaac, and Jacob are regarded as grandfather, father, and son: immediately succeeding generations within one family. Yet because of the longevity with which they are credited, their three generations amount to something like 400 years. When discussions of a 'patriarchal age' arise, it is important to establish whether what is envisaged is the lifespan of three individuals—say, 100–150 years—or a period extending up to 400 years. In the first case it is very improbable that one family should have left any trace in history, and we must simply regard the stories as family traditions of uncertain date. In the second case, alleged parallels from the ancient Near East over an extended period may be brought into the discussion, but we then have to acknowledge that we are a very long way from the biblical account itself.

   This ambiguity is only one reason among those which lead many scholars to be sceptical as to the possibility of treating the Genesis material as historical in any modern sense of the term. Even among those who are prepared to see a historical nucleus in these stories, there is no consensus of opinion as to their precise historical context or even their appropriate social setting. At times, the impression created by the Genesis stories is that Abraham and Jacob were wanderers, moving with their flocks and herds from place to place (Gen. 13: 1–7; 37: 12–17); in other passages they appear to be associated with particular settlements, especially with regard to religious practice (Gen. 22: 19; 35: 27). Further despite the statement that 'at that time the Canaanites were in the land' (Gen. 12: 6)—itself often regarded as a sign of much later editorial comment—there is in the main body of Genesis stories virtually no sign of other inhabitants of the land save the main participants. This in itself is an indication that we are in the realm of family tradition rather than anything which would normally be recognized as history. Nowhere is any indication found of the flourishing civilizations known to have existed in Palestine during much of the second millennium BC.

It seems most probable, therefore, that these stories should either be regarded as wholly the products of a later age, made up at a time when it was felt necessary to satisfy curiosity about the origins of the nation, or, perhaps more plausibly, that ancient traditions have been preserved but rearranged and reshaped in the light of the religious and theological presuppositions of a later age. On one specific issue there is much dispute among scholars, with no likelihood of any agreement in the near future. This concerns the question of 'parallels', that is to say, social and legal customs referred to in the book of Genesis which are alleged to show similarities with such customs elsewhere in the ancient Near East. There can be no doubt that too often study of the book of Genesis has taken insufficient account of what was known of the surrounding world during possibly contemporary ages, but equally there has been evidence of the opposite tendency: each possible link with the ancient Near East being hailed as proof that the Bible has been shown to be 'true'. This issue will come up for consideration again when the contribution of archaeology to Old Testament study is considered (see below, ch. 4).

Creation and flood

The most famous of these supposed 'proofs' of the truth of the biblical record was the discovery by C. L. (later Sir Leonard) Woolley, in the 1920s, of evidence of a devastating flood at Ur, the 'Ur of the Chaldees' from which Abraham is said to have set out on his journey to Palestine (Gen. 11: 31). Reference to the flood brings us to the last of the four periods set apart for our consideration. In fact, little attention need be given here to the material in Genesis 1–11. It fulfils none of the criteria which would be necessary for a modern historian to regard it as historical, and only the preconceived notion that everything in the Bible must necessarily be factually accurate could have led to any other conclusion. We shall therefore ignore at this point the stories of creation and 'fall', of universal flood and of confusion of language, though to do so is in no way to dismiss the importance of these stories, or of the lessons contained in them. (By way of postscript, it may be noted that the flood levels at Ur, dramatic though they were, represented only a local inundation; excavations at other sites soon dispelled any idea of a universal flood.)

The importance of history

This somewhat breathless account of the problems concerning the historicity of the early books of the Old Testament is intended as a preliminary to the more basic question of the importance of history in Old Testament study. The historical approach has often been elevated so as to have an almost mystical significance; Judaism and Christianity have regularly been spoken of as 'historical religions', and the assertion is made that the events of which they speak 'really happened', with the clear implication that they are thereby sharply differentiated from other, particularly Eastern, religious traditions.

It will readily be seen that many questions are raised by this approach, not all of which can be discussed here. An expression once frequently found was 'sacred history', which in effect amounted to a claim that the Bible was exempt from the usual criteria of scholarly accuracy and precision. Such a claim would not now be seriously entertained, but the view of Judaism and

Christianity as in a unique sense 'historical religions' has meant that various attempts have been made to present the truth of the biblical account as being some special kind of history. Thus, for example, the German word *Heilsgeschichte*, sometimes translated as 'salvation history', has been much used as part of a claim that certain events described in the Bible have a particular status as *both* historical events *and* examples of God's saving power at work. In particular, as far as the Old Testament is concerned, the Exodus, the deliverance from Egypt, has been seen as *the* characteristic salvation-historical event. Certainly the large number of references and allusions to the Exodus throughout the Old Testament makes it clear that Israel's faith in its God was in a special way bound up with the belief that he had delivered them from the oppressive power of Egyptian bondage.

It is when consideration is given to the exact sense in which this event is to be described as historical that difficulties arise. The whole idea of history 'as it actually happened' is notoriously problematic, since every event, trivial or of international dimensions, will be interpreted in very different ways by different witnesses. How true this is in the case of the Exodus we have already seen earlier in this chapter, and it is noteworthy that, whereas much energy was expended by scholars of an earlier generation in trying to establish the route of the Exodus, the identity of the ruling Pharaoh, and all the accompanying 'historical' details, the more recent tendency is to accept both that such details are unattainable and, more significantly for our present discussion, that they are not of major importance. If that is indeed so, then the claim to historicity is, it will be seen, a claim of a very unusual kind.

Quite a different series of problems arises from the way in which a historically governed method of approach has shaped the perception of many aspects of the Old Testament. One very obvious example would be the books of Chronicles, much of whose content is paralleled in Samuel-Kings. The Chronicler is the later writer, and where his account differs from that in Samuel-Kings, much argument has centred around the question whether these differences can be given a historical explanation, rather than any attempt to understand what the Chronicler was actually saying. But since Chronicles is likely to be one of the lesser-known parts of the Old

Testament, more familiar examples can be found in the books of the prophets. It is a standard concern (and in some extreme cases almost the only one) in commentaries and introductions to attempt to trace how much of each book goes back to the prophet after whom it is named and how far the historical circumstances of his time are reflected. If Amos, for example, is to be regarded primarily as a witness to the social and economic conditions of eighth-century Israel, then it is clearly of fundamental importance to eliminate any material in the book which comes from a later period. But it is at least arguable that to approach Amos in this way is to be guilty of a misconception. What we know of Amos is a book, and that collection should surely be the primary object of study. Indeed, some would go further, and say that Amos ought to be regarded as an important 'chapter' in a larger book, the collection of the twelve Minor Prophets, and that to rearrange these prophetic 'chapters' in their supposed historical order is to miss an important part of their collective impact.

Two examples from the book of Amos will illustrate these points. The first main section of the book (1: 3–2: 16) consists of a series of oracles against foreign nations, aimed at each of Israel's neighbours in turn, and ending with a dramatic outburst against Israel itself. The details of some of these oracles have often been called in evidence for the political and economic circumstances of the time, both in their specific attacks and in their silences—for example, the fact that no reference is made to Assyria, whose threat became acute a few years after the time of Amos. It is almost universally agreed by scholars that the oracle against Judah (2: 4–5) is a later addition. Its form lacks some of the features of the basic collection, and its content is much more vague and generalized than the vivid denunciations characteristic of the oracles against Damascus (1: 3–5) or the Ammonites (1: 13–15). By contrast, the condemnation of Judah states simply that

> they have rejected the law of the LORD
> and have not kept his statutes.

From expressions of this kind it is impossible to deduce any particular historical setting, and very often the result has been that this particular oracle has been passed over with little comment.

In fact it is possible to argue that the introduction of an oracle aimed against Judah in a collection which reached its present form in Judah is of extreme importance. If our concern in studying Amos were simply to discover the state of affairs among the smaller nations of Syria-Palestine in the mid-eighth century BC, it could be disregarded. But the Old Testament is the text of a continuing religious community, and that is shown by the fact that the prophet's words, originally directed against the northern kingdom of Israel, were not thought to have lost all their relevance when that kingdom was destroyed. God's words through Amos were still of importance in totally different circumstances. It was the same God who had warned Israel through the words of his prophet who would bring a comparable fate upon Judah. 'The strongholds of Jerusalem' were just as liable to be destroyed as had been those of Tyre (1: 10) or of Bozrah in Edom (1: 12). This readiness to update the prophetic words showed that they were not simply tied to one historical situation; they had a continuing effectiveness in quite different conditions.

A second example will illustrate in a rather different way the point that a purely historical approach, with its concern solely for what is original to the prophet himself, is inadequate for the proper study of Amos. After the dire threats which have characterized most of the book, the optimism of the last few verses (9: 8*b*–15) comes as a great surprise. Though a few scholars have tried to maintain the originality of these verses on the grounds that an alternation of oracles of judgement and of promise is characteristic of Hebrew prophecy, the contrast with what has preceded is here so great that almost all commentators have come to the conclusion that they must represent an addition from a later period, and the reference to 'the booth of David that is fallen' (9: 11) has persuaded most that the addition must presuppose the downfall of the southern kingdom of Judah and the exile of its leading inhabitants, including the Davidic rulers (2 Kgs. 24: 14–16).

At the historical level, however, there are few clues as to the setting of this material, and a purely historical approach has tended to dismiss it as the over-optimistic imaginings of a later editor. A more constructive way of looking at this passage may be to see it as forming an important link in the putting together of the whole

'Book of the Twelve', that is, the Minor Prophets. Just as the beginning of Amos shows links with the book of Joel which precedes it (cf. Amos 1: 2 with Joel 3: 16 in particular), so the end of Amos provides a link with the book of Obadiah which follows it. Amos has warned that even God's own chosen people cannot expect to avoid God's inevitable judgement. But that is not the whole of the story. Eventually God promises that he will restore the house of David 'as in the days of old' (Amos 9: 11), so that

> they may possess the remnant of Edom,
>   and all the nations who are called by my name.

This promise for Israel/threat for her enemies thus provides a link with Obadiah, in which verses 1–14 are concerned with spelling out the fate of Edom, and verses 15–21 that of 'all the nations'. The context, as in Amos 9: 11, is 'the day of the LORD' (Obad. 15), pictured here as a day of God's judgement upon all his enemies. This fuller development only makes sense if Amos and Obadiah are looked at together, yet because the actual individual prophets lived at different epochs, Amos in the eighth century, Obadiah probably in the sixth, a purely historical approach all too often ignores this link.

Story

A third limitation of the purely historical approach, and one that has been much discussed in recent years, is the relation between history and story. In so far as the Old Testament is historical it is overwhelmingly because it contains many narratives which appear to relate to historical events and persons; other types of historical evidence, such as archives or official records, are rarely present. The lists of court officials in 2 Samuel 8: 16–18 and elsewhere may provide a partial exception; more frequently we find references to official annals which have not survived (e.g. 1 Kgs. 11: 41, and often elsewhere in the books of Kings). But the extensive narrative material in the Old Testament has regularly been understood as if it were, and were intended to be, historical. Yet much of the material that is in such a form would be almost universally rejected as history if the usual criteria for historicity were to be applied. Sometimes this rejection would be due to the sheer implausibility of what is asserted, as for example the age of the characters involved, or the intervention of heavenly beings, or the contravention of what we should regard as the 'natural order'. Where none of these difficulties arises, an event, though plausible enough in itself, may yet lack the kind of supporting evidence which we should regard as essential for true historicity. Often, for example, we come across private conversations which are a significant feature of the story-teller's art, but are not to be taken seriously as true history. The conversation between Ahab and Jezebel in the story of Naboth's vineyard (1 Kgs. 21: 5–7) would be a good example; the demands of the story are such that something of the kind 'must have happened'; it is not in any normal sense of the word 'historical'. Too often vividness of detail has been assumed to imply also historical accuracy and precision.

It is also relevant at this point to note that for many readers the instinctive—and surely entirely proper—reaction to much Old Testament material is to treasure it as story without any direct concern as to historical reliability. The beautiful account of the courtship of Rebekah (Gen. 24); the adventures of Joseph in Egypt (Gen. 37, 39–50); the fall of Jericho (Josh. 2–6); the escapades of Samson (Judg. 13–16): these and many more examples, familiar, no doubt, to many readers, owe their impact to their literary quality as stories, and historical issues can only be regarded as irrelevant detail. There is no need to return to a 'Bible stories' intellectual level to recognize the importance of story as a literary category in its own right.

It will be noted that these examples of story all come from the material which we considered earlier in this chapter, noting the difficulties involved in treating it as historical. This has an important implication for the use of history in Old Testament study. If the books from Genesis (or at least Gen. 12 onwards) to Judges are approached mainly as history, there will be a natural expectation that this material and extra-biblical discoveries will, as it were, support one another, each throwing light on the other to enable the overall historical picture to become clearer. So, for example, it has often been supposed that various Mesopotamian texts might help us to identify a historical period which might legitimately be called 'the patriarchal age', just as Genesis might help in the decipherment of newly found extra-biblical texts.

Despite various claims, however, it seems doubtful whether such a relation of mutual support actually exists. That is to say, the stories of Abraham and Jacob, of Moses and Joshua, and of the judges may indeed contain ancient elements; but they have not been handed down with an antiquarian concern to preserve those details accurately, and so their historical reliability in any modern sense is very dubious. From this angle also, that is to say, the difficulties noted earlier in this chapter are reinforced.

One last point may be mentioned as yet further illustration of the fact that the predominantly historical approach to the Old Testament is coming under scrutiny for a variety of reasons. This arises from the fact that perceptions of history among professional historians are changing very considerably. No longer can it be considered axiomatic that a narrative embodying great men and events adds up to a history; all kinds of other evidence must be brought into the total picture. But scholarly works entitled 'History of Israel' still for the most part consist of a retelling of the story in the biblical books, modified only by reference to other material of similar type from other ancient Near Eastern sources. Economic, social, climatological, and other considerations play at most only a marginal part. Developments within the discipline of history almost certainly mean that the history of Israel and the study of the 'historical' texts of the Old Testament must stand as distinct disciplines.

In a sense this recognition coincides with the acknowledgement both that there are parts of the Old Testament—the Psalms, Job, Proverbs, for example—which are not susceptible to historical questioning, and that too great a concern with historical issues can obscure other important insights into the more apparently historical texts. Just as a sensitive reading of the Old Testament needs to view the prophetic books as literary wholes, and not simply to discard those sections commonly regarded as later additions, so it needs also to recognize the importance and value of story as a medium without having constantly to ask whether or not the narrative is an accurate historical account.

All this is in no way either to denigrate the way in which historical study of the Old Testament has contributed to our present understanding, or to suggest that that form of study is a thing of the past. In many ways the present situation is once again a result of that explosion of knowledge to which reference has several times been made. The study of the history of Israel, even if it be confined to the political level, is now a complex discipline, involving a variety of interlocking skills, and it is no longer possible simply to regard it as a retelling of the Old Testament story with a few extra-biblical texts thrown in. As with English medieval history we can no longer be content to regard it as simply a series of good kings and bad kings. The Old Testament remains a prime source of historical knowledge; it is not in itself primarily a history book.

These cautions with regard to the historical approach might seem to go clean contrary to one very obvious fact: the enormous popular interest in archaeology in general and 'biblical archaeology' in particular. Here surely is an area which must be regarded as a tremendous support to a primarily historical understanding? In any case the interest in archaeology is so great, the explosion of knowledge so remarkable, and, we must say, confusion so widespread, that it is clearly a topic which demands a chapter to itself.

4

What does Archaeology Contribute?

For more than a century it has been taken for granted that our knowledge of the Bible, and of the Old Testament in particular, is enhanced by the many archaeological discoveries which have taken place, not only in Palestine itself, but also in the whole area of the ancient Near East which constitutes the biblical world. It is a subject which has generated a great deal of popular interest, as is witnessed by the television programmes devoted to it, and the wide range of books of every degree of difficulty. There was a time when archaeology was little more than 'treasure-hunting', digging a promising site so as to find and take away as many attractive monuments, statues, and the like, as possible. Now, not only do local governments very properly object to the despoliation of their own inheritance, but also a more scientific approach to the whole subject ensures that the significance of an archaeological excavation goes far beyond mere 'finds'; the whole pattern of life of the inhabitants of the site being explored will come under scrutiny.

In addition to the increased technical expertise of modern archaeological work, there is another consideration which is of direct relevance. The early impetus toward archaeology in Palestine in particular, and to a large extent in surrounding countries, came from the desire to 'prove' the truth of the biblical record in face of the attacks being mounted upon it by what was termed 'higher criticism', that is, detailed source-critical study whose results were often regarded as excessively negative. In such circumstances the use of the term 'biblical archaeology' was natural, and gave a clear indication of the particular concerns of those involved in the work. Some work of this kind, financed by religious groups, still continues, but to an increasing extent archaeology has become a scientific and a dispassionate means of enquiry into the past of humanity; it can no longer be regarded simply as a 'handmaiden' to biblical (or any other) studies.

The larger setting

The setting of the Old Testament is to an overwhelming extent Palestine, and so it is ironical that many of the most important archaeological contributions to our knowledge of the Old Testament come, not from Palestine at all, but from other parts of the ancient Near East. The reasons for this, and its implications, are so important that they need to be set out straightaway.

For the most part discoveries in Palestine itself have been a part of what is sometimes called 'mute' archaeology. That is to say, sites have been excavated, occupation layers established, cultural patterns clarified; but very rarely has there been any accompanying literary evidence to set alongside discoveries of this kind. Only at Qumran, near the Dead Sea, has a major collection of texts been unearthed, and they came from the very last centuries BC, so that in many ways they shed more light on the background of the New Testament than on the Old Testament. (On the importance of these Dead Sea Scrolls for our understanding of the *text* of the Old Testament, see above, ch. 2). From the period before 200 BC, by contrast, the literary evidence that has emerged is of the most fragmentary kind: a few inscribed seals, a brief inscription in the 'Siloam Tunnel' near Jerusalem, a crudely carved 'calendar' setting out the agricultural activities of different periods of the year, fragments of letters from the time of the Babylonian invasion, and, from the later period, coins. (Only the recently discovered inscriptions from Kuntillet Ajrud, which we shall look at again when considering religious developments, offer an exception here.) Matter of this kind, interesting though it is to specialists, is scarcely likely to play a major part in building up our knowledge of the setting of the Old Testament. From Palestine itself, therefore, we are confined almost exclusively to the conclusions that can be drawn from the various sites that have been excavated.

By contrast to this the remainder of the Near East has provided a rich body of textual evidence. From Egypt come the Tell el-Amarna letters, first discovered in the nineteenth century; from modern Iraq, excavations at Mari and Nuzi have provided extensive collections of legal, administrative, and religious documents; from Ras Shamra, in modern Syria, the ancient Ugarit, come texts in a language closely akin to Hebrew; also in Syria, the more recent excavations at Tell Mardik, the ancient Ebla, have shown a high level of civilization dating back to the third millennium BC. The significance of these, and of some of the other finds, is still being clarified.

None of these places is mentioned in the Bible, and none of the texts that have originated from these sites makes any reference to biblical characters or events. There have been other excavations, however, which have enabled scholars to provide more precise correlations with the biblical traditions. In particular, as we saw in the last chapter, the historical annals of the Assyrian and Babylonian empires enable us to fill out in considerable detail the impact of these empires upon Israel and Judah, from the eighth to the sixth centuries BC. To an overwhelming extent the broad outline of the biblical account, especially that in 2 Kings, is confirmed, even though particular details have needed to be modified or reassessed. Thus, to take an extreme example, it is claimed that it is now possible to identify the very day on which the army of Nebuchadnezzar accepted the surrender of Jerusalem: 15 March 597 BC (cf. 2 Kgs. 24: 12).

The contribution of archaeology: a real world

These preliminary considerations should already make it clear that the contribution of archaeology to our understanding of the Old Testament is not an univocal one; at least four different types of relation need to be borne in mind. First, and in most general terms, there is the very positive contribution made by the way in which archaeological discoveries can demonstrate that it was a real world in which the men and women of the Old (and New) Testament lived their lives. Very often the stories of the Bible have such haunting power that they tend to be divorced from historical reality;

archaeological discoveries remind us of the danger and loss involved in such a divorce. To take but one example: the story of Jacob's sons going into Egypt to buy food because of the famine in Palestine (Gen. 42–3). The same cycle of stories tells of Midianite and Ishmaelite traders passing through Palestine on their way into Egypt (Gen. 37; 39). Wall-reliefs from royal tombs at Beni Hasan, on the Nile, depict Semitic groups deferentially approaching the Pharaoh. There is no suggestion that those depicted should be identified with the family of Jacob, for the Beni Hasan paintings are much earlier than any conceivable date for Joseph and his brothers; indeed, in the strict sense nothing is said about historicity, for the story of Jacob's family could have been a kind of historical novel, based on well-known custom. The point is rather that, whether or not the biblical account be factual, we are given a new perspective in our understanding. It is a bonus comparable to that experienced by many travellers from Europe or the USA going to the Holy Land for the first time and seeing for themselves the reality underlying many of the familiar place-names.

Historical links

The second contribution of archaeology is equally positive, and has already been hinted at. From the middle of the ninth century BC onwards for more than two hundred years, Israel and Judah played a part on the world stage. More or less detailed correlations are available, as a result of excavations at different sites in modern Iraq which in the ancient world were associated with the Assyrian or Babylonian empires. Many of the artefacts discovered in these excavations, together with accompanying literary texts, are now in the British Museum, in London, and it is possible there to gain a vivid picture of the distinctive features of a particular ancient civilization. The Assyrian material is especially striking. The Israelite king Jehu (mentioned in 2 Kgs. 9–10) is depicted on an obelisk, grovelling before his superior; the acceptance by Hezekiah king of Judah of ignominious terms imposed upon him by Sennacherib of Assyria is described in an extended display inscription. Here a brief account in 2 Kings 18: 13–16 seems to correlate very closely with the Assyrian version of events; by contrast the more extended account in 2 Kings 18: 17–19: 37, according to which the outcome was much more favourable to Judah, offers an example of a tension between biblical and extra-biblical sources of information. It will remain a matter for dispute whether this more extended biblical account contains a historical nucleus; in any case we are warned not to expect precise confirmation of one source of information by another as a general rule.

This close correlation comes to an end, in any case, with the beginning of the Persian period. We have already seen (ch. 3) that historical information for that period from the Old Testament itself is very scanty, and the quantity of relevant archaeological data is also reduced. Cyrus, the Persian ruler who conquered Babylon, is favourably referred to in the Old Testament (Isa. 44: 28; 45: 1; Ezra 1) and the 'Cyrus Cylinder' has often been interpreted as introducing a policy of greater enlightenment and tolerance than that of the Assyrians and Babylonians, though it is far from clear that such an interpretation is correct. Relevant also for our understanding of Judaism are the Elephantine papyri, found in Egypt. But once again the evidence from Palestine itself is virtually non-existent. Alexander the Great, one of the most remarkable figures in the history of the ancient world, passed through Palestine on his path of conquest, yet he remains unmentioned in the canonical Old Testament, and it is to Josephus, the Jewish historian writing in the first century AD, that we have to turn for information about his relations with the Jews.

This second type of contribution of archaeology to our understanding of the Old Testament is an important one, and should certainly be recognized as such. A limitation does, however, arise from the fact that this is precisely the kind of Old Testament material about which historical difficulties are unlikely to be felt. That Israel and Judah *were* nation-states in the period from the tenth to the sixth centuries BC, ruled over by the kings named in 1 and 2 Kings, would scarcely be challenged by even the most sceptical, so that archaeological corroboration in this area, though of very great interest, does not of itself add a new dimension to our existing knowledge.

A 'patriarchal age'?

It is when we come to the third type of evidence that difficulties emerge. This evidence relates to the period which, as we saw in the previous chapter, gives rise to problems of historical reconstruction, that is to say, the time before the establishment of the monarchy under David and Solomon. In particular, the question arises whether texts discovered in Mesopotamia or in Egypt can legitimately be held to contribute to our knowledge of the historical background of Genesis and, to a lesser extent, Exodus. There have not been wanting claims during the last half-century that such a contribution is indeed available. In particular, it has been maintained that excavations at Mari on the River Euphrates, and at Nuzi on the Tigris, have revealed texts which provide a clear and plausible background against which the wanderings of the patriarchs Abraham, Isaac, and Jacob could be set. To be still more specific it has often been alleged that the extensive collection of legal material from Nuzi throws a great deal of light on otherwise unexplained social customs to which reference is made in the book of Genesis, but which seem to find no place elsewhere in the Old Testament. Thus, the curious story of the patriarch passing off his wife as his sister, found three times in Genesis (chs. 12, 20, and 26) has been thought to be illustrated by a supposed Nuzi custom according to which, upon marriage, a woman could be spoken of as the 'sister', as well as the wife, of a man. Again, the elaborate arrangements made by Abraham concerning inheritance when it appeared that his wife was likely to remain childless (Gen. 15 and 16) have been compared to arrangements made in allegedly similar circumstances in the Nuzi texts.

Older studies of Genesis made much of these alleged 'parallels', and argued that in their light we could be confident in our identification of a 'patriarchal age'. The claim has never seriously been made that specific reference to Abraham or to Jacob could be found in these ancient sources; rather, it was held that the society and its customs underlying these texts provided a uniquely congenial context into which the stories of the patriarchs could be placed.

It was a little disconcerting, however, to observe that, even among those who took such a view, there was no agreement as to when that 'patriarchal age' might have been, since different archaeological discoveries related to different periods, and were given different weight by scholars. Thus, for some, references to ethnic movements in texts dating from around 2000 BC were of prime significance, and it was in such a context at such a period that Abraham's migration from 'Ur of the Chaldees' and Haran (Gen. 11: 31–12: 4) was to be placed. For others, the details of personal names in the Mari texts from the eighteenth century BC were more important, and the patriarchs were dated at that period. For others again, the Nuzi legal texts of about the fifteenth century provided particular illumination; for yet others it was the Tell el-Amarna archive from Egypt, with its references to unsettled conditions in Palestine in the fourteenth century, that provided the appropriate context.

Such variety is, to say the least, disturbing, if historical background is being sought. It has led to a greater reluctance among recent scholars to suppose that archaeological discoveries of this kind can shed any *direct* light on the Old Testament. All would agree that they supply valuable indirect testimony, telling us much about the kind of world from which Israel's ancestors may have emerged. Not least important is the high degree of civilization to which they bear testimony. From all these sources, and from others not mentioned here, the picture which emerges is a remarkably sophisticated one. Active trade between different states was carried on; there was full-scale diplomatic activity, an established bureaucracy and governmental system. Any suggestion of 'primitive' or 'savage' modes of life should be firmly set aside. In religious practice there are clear signs of developed systems of belief, so that here too the thought of the worship of 'sticks and stones' sometimes implied in older treatments of the patriarchs is quite inappropriate. Yet all of this evidence relates to the Genesis stories in only an indirect way, for no evidence has emerged which would enable us to establish any precise historical setting in which the ancestors of Israel could be placed.

Excavations in Palestine

In this area of discussion no reference has been made to any Palestinian sites. They provide the context for the fourth, and in many ways the most controversial, kind of relation between archaeological discoveries and the Old Testament. The difficulties relate for the most part less to the patriarchal period than to the events described in the books of Joshua and Judges, which picture the settlement of Israel in Palestine. It is of this material that many will automatically think when 'biblical archaeology' is mentioned, for everyone has heard of, say, the story of Jericho, where the walls came tumbling down, and will naturally ask whether archaeological excavations have been able to shed any light on that story as told in Joshua 6, or on the accounts of the capture of other cities, in particular Ai (Josh. 7–8). The following chapters of Joshua refer to a number of other cities in the south and the north of the land also said to have been captured by the invading Israelites, though in these instances the story is told with much less detail.

It is at this point that difficulties start to be found. Broadly speaking they are of three kinds. First, there are in a number of cases uncertainties as to the actual identification of particular sites. Secondly, there are complications of dating and stratigraphy: with how much confidence may the evidence discovered by excavation be correlated with possibly relevant literary material? Thirdly, and dependent upon the second point, what is to be done when no apparently satisfactory correlation emerges from the comparison of archaeological and literary evidence? All these questions, though distinct in principle, are often closely intertwined in practice.

First, then, the identification of particular sites. In some instances, of course, no problem arises. In Jerusalem, for example, the identity of the site has never been obscured, owing to the political and religious importance of the city through the centuries. Though the main occupational area shifted even during biblical times, the 'city of David' being further south than the area developed by his successors, no question arises as to the identity of the site. The actual extent of the city during different parts of the biblical period remains a much-debated question, as does the precise relation of Israelite Jerusalem to the earlier Canaanite city occupied by the Jebusites, with which it is identified in Joshua 18: 28, but some at least of these problems are being resolved by current Israeli excavations.

In other places, though the ancient city may not have been in precisely the same position as the modern one, a tradition of more or less continuous occupation removes any serious doubt. Jericho would here be a good case in point. The ancient settlement has been extensively excavated; it is not in the same position as either the modern city or New Testament Jericho, but its identification is beyond serious question. There may be instances where a modern, usually Arabic, place-name may provide an important clue: El-jib, for example, is confidently identified with biblical Gibeon. But not too much confidence can be placed in associations of this kind; such links are often not so securely established as their general acceptance might seem to imply. ('Cana in Galilee' and Emmaus are two New Testament examples of such disputed identifications.)

When all possible links of this kind have been evaluated, there still remains a very large number of place-names referred to in the Old Testament which cannot be confidently identified with any specific modern site. Equally, there have been many sites at which archaeological excavation has been carried out and remains from the Old Testament period discovered, without any sure grounds for a precise identification. Two examples, out of many possibilities, may be used as illustrations.

In south-western Palestine, a large-scale excavation was carried out between 1926 and 1932 on a site called Tell beit-Mirsim. In many ways the work was a model of its kind, pioneering new scientific techniques. The modern name of the site does not correspond to any that is mentioned in the Bible, yet the discovery of extensive Bronze Age settlement made it likely that it must have been a place of importance during at least some parts of the biblical period. For many years, partly because of the very strong claims put forward by its distinguished excavator, the late W. F. Albright, it was thought that Tell beit-Mirsim could be identified with biblical Debir, reference to whose capture by the Israelites is found in Joshua 10: 38f. More recent studies have, however, given rise to very serious doubts as to the correctness of this identification, which is no longer generally maintained. We are thus left with two unknowns: the modern site of biblical Debir, and the possible biblical identification of Tell beit-Mirsim. This example is unusual only in that a particular, and probably mistaken, identification was so long upheld. There are many other artificial mounds ('tells') which might contain valuable information but have never been excavated; there are many biblical settlements whose identification is either quite unknown or at best disputed.

Our second example relating to site-identification concerns Ai, which, as we have seen, is of major significance in the story of Joshua's conquest (Josh. 7–8). The biblical 'placing' of Ai is unusually precise (Gen. 12: 8; Josh. 7: 2), and it has long been maintained that a specific site, Et-tell, should be identified with biblical Ai. But Et-tell has been thoroughly excavated, and it is clear that it was not inhabited on any extensive scale at any possible date for Joshua, since the main occupation had come to an end in the third millennium BC. Here it will be seen that difficulties arise! Some have claimed that the identification, Et-tell=Ai, must be a wrong one; others have argued for a confusion in the account, between Ai and neighbouring Bethel; others again have thought in terms of a small-scale settlement which the excavators failed to discover or which left no traces. Probably the majority of scholars would maintain, however, that all of these suggestions are unsatisfactory expedients, and that the account in Joshua cannot be taken as a historical narrative. The word 'Ai' means 'ruin', and at least one element in the story is likely to have been aetiological, that is to say, an attempt to give an explanation of the origin of a prominent ruin and, in particular, to associate that with the heroic progress of Israel's conquest of the land. If this is so, archaeology still has an important part to play in helping us to understand the Old Testament, but not quite in the sense of correlation between excavation and text which is normally envisaged.

Identification of a site, however, does not remove all problems. A second type of difficulty relates to dating and stratigraphy. Modern archaeological investigation will not wish to confine itself to those matters which are of interest to the student of the Old Testament: as we shall see at the end of this chapter, a whole range of expertise will be brought to bear upon a wide variety of evidence. In one sense, of course, this additional information is most welcome as shedding more light on the biblical period, but difficulties are also caused. Thus, it is clear that many Palestinian sites reveal evidence of severe devastation in the late Bronze Age, perhaps around 1200

BC (though archaeologists are cautious about translating the 'ages' with which they work into precise dates). But it would be a contradiction of sound archaeological method simply to concentrate on that one block of evidence to the exclusion of all else, and to claim that this devastation must have been brought about by the invading Israelites. In a larger context it becomes clear that every archaeological period produced its devastation; that we often have no means of differentiating between destruction brought about by natural causes (fire or earthquake) and that which was the result of enemy action; and that even when enemy action does seem likely the enemy might as probably be the inhabitants of a neighbouring city as foreign invaders.

In this connection it has sometimes been claimed that one feature which may enable us to identify an Israelite presence is the fact that at many sites Late Bronze Age remains display a lower cultural level than that characteristic of earlier periods. It is then alleged that this points to the arrival of semi-nomadic groups from the desert fringes displacing the earlier and more civilized (in terms of material culture) Canaanite inhabitants. It may be so; but it is now clear that this lower cultural level was a more widespread phenomenon, not confined to Palestine, and so well beyond the range of any possible Israelite settlement. Other causes, such as changes in climate, could underlie this phenomenon; the settlement of the Israelites in Palestine is certainly not in itself an adequate explanation.

Finally, there is the problem of the lack of correlation between literary and archaeological evidence. This point has already been touched upon to some extent in the discussion of Ai, but the classical example of the dilemma which is posed is Jericho. Here there is no dispute about the site. When 'Jericho' is referred to in ancient texts, it is modern Tell es-Sultan, a little to the north-west of the modern city, that is intended. Nor can there be any dispute as to the importance of the city in the account of the Israelites' arrival in the Promised Land: Joshua 2–6 is a story which reaches a climax with the capture of Jericho. It is therefore entirely natural that great interest should have been taken in the excavation of the site, and it is one of the most fully explored of all Palestinian sites. In the years between the two world wars it seemed as if the walls of the city destroyed by Joshua had been identified, the only problem being that this destruction had taken place at a date significantly earlier than that which otherwise seemed most likely for the Israelites' entry into Canaan. However, during the 1950s and 1960s, further excavations, using more modern techniques, demonstrated that the previously proposed identification could not be maintained, and that there was in fact no certain trace of any settlement during any plausible period for Joshua. Here, that is to say, the same problem arose as that relating to Ai, but with additional complications. At Jericho there was no possibility of supposing that the wrong site had been identified, and the extremely elaborate account of the capture of Jericho in the book of Joshua ruled out any ambiguity. Though there are still some who argue that the biblical account must retain a historical nucleus—perhaps a small settlement all traces of which have been lost—the great majority of scholars has now come to acknowledge that, if archaeology is to be allowed to make its contribution, it speaks decisively against the historicity of Joshua's capture of Jericho.

Does this mean that the contribution of archaeology to Old Testament study is overwhelmingly negative? That its real importance only arises when it *dis*proves some apparently historical account? At one level it might seem so; but this is almost certainly not the whole story. To a considerable extent this negative impression is created by the very nature of the questions being put to the archaeologist. If, as has often been the case, archaeology is simply used as a tool which may be helpful when it appears to corroborate the historicity of the biblical record, then it will be a dangerously double-edged weapon. There will be many instances of the kind we have just been considering, where the archaeological evidence, far from corroborating the biblical picture, suggests that the events described cannot be historical at all. Indeed, we might say that to use archaeology in this way is to invite disappointment, for apparently positive correlations can never be established with complete confidence, whereas negative verdicts are usually final. It could never have been proved that the apparent evidence of Joshua's wall was indeed that; discovery that a site was unoccupied at a particular period is most unlikely to be changed by further investigation.

It can therefore be seen that the relation between literary study of the Bible and archaeology is always likely to be an uneasy one. It is significant that archaeologists now for the most part object to the expression 'biblical archaeology'. Their discipline is one that has its own intrinsic importance and value; like the other fields of study mentioned at the beginning of this book, it has undergone an explosion of knowledge, and its current interest and expertise has shifted a great deal from the concentration on 'discoveries' of which we have for the most part been talking.

The new archaeology

To a great extent archaeology is now concerned less with 'finds' than with the application of a whole range of scientific and technological expertise to understanding and reconstructing the life of a particular society. That life will be explored in all its aspects, social and economic, religious and political, and attention will also be given to the larger context within which that life was lived: climatic changes, characteristic flora and fauna of the region, and so on. Such a discipline must inevitably set its horizons much more widely than the particular geographical area or historical period described in the biblical record, but for the student of ancient Israel it can be the more valuable for that.

At this point a tension arises similar to that which we have already noted in our consideration of the value of history for our study of the Old Testament. Just as increasing sophistication of historical method seems to weaken the long-established links between the history of ancient Israel and the biblical stories, so something analogous is happening with archaeology. Its range of reference is increasing; no longer can it be confined to the illustration of the biblical accounts. Less a series of sensational 'discoveries' (though they may still occur), more the gradual unfolding of a map of ancient society in which the biblical people had their own limited but significant role—that would appear to be the role of archaeology *vis-à-vis* biblical study.

To make such a suggestion is to make another assumption which would in the past have been vigorously challenged. Discussions of this kind assume that ancient Israel was a society comparable in all its significant aspects with other contemporary societies, a society whose political, economic, and social structures can legitimately be set alongside and compared with those of her neighbours, and illuminated by the work of archaeologists. But already the assumptions involved in statements of this kind have far-reaching implications, for they take for granted that Israel was a society essentially similar to the surrounding peoples. It is to the propriety of that assumption that we must next turn our attention.

5

What Kind of Society was Israel?

The potential value of archaeology for a better understanding of the Old Testament has been recognized for more than a century; any formal contribution from sociology, by contrast, has been a much more recent development and is, so far, of much more modest dimensions. That situation is, however, already changing, and in a number of ways it has come to be recognized that the understanding of the actual society which constituted ancient Israel can be very significant for many aspects of Old Testament study.

The social context of the Old Testament

The first point of application of such an understanding relates to the social standpoint of the Old Testament books themselves. Who were their writers? To whom were they addressed? Now at one level these questions are unanswerable. It is most unlikely that we shall ever know in any precise historical sense the circumstances of composition of particular books. But, whereas the historian is characteristically concerned with exact and precise answers, the sociologist is more interested in the general and typical, and so it may still be useful to gain an overview.

We may say that the books of the Old Testament are by and large the products of the upper strata of society. In the classical world, and probably also in the Old Testament, the establishment and development of historical traditions was the work of an intellectual élite, not simply the product of a generalized popular process. It is probable that literacy was itself the preserve of a relatively small group; and again it is noteworthy that when, for example, servants or slaves are referred to, it is always assumed that the hearers or readers would be those who might themselves possess such servants, rather than that they would be members of the servant class. Thus, for example, in the Ten Commandments, the requirement of Sabbath rest is addressed to the full member of the Israelite community, but also to his (and the masculine form is deliberately chosen) menservants and maidservants (Exod. 20: 10), and in the slightly variant form of the Commandments found in Deuteronomy this is elaborated along the lines of a humanitarian appeal to the ruling class: 'that your manservant and your maidservant may rest as well as you' (Deut. 5: 14). Similarly the book of Proverbs and some of the prophetic collections, notably Isaiah, make reference to the king and the royal court in terms which make it clear that the compilers had ready access to the highest ranks in the land.

To whom were prophetic oracles or wisdom sayings addressed? This question is less easy to answer. Sometimes an individual is the target of a prophetic oracle, and when that is so the individual is again characteristically the king or a member of his entourage, such as Shebna, the royal steward (Isa. 22: 15). More frequently it is impossible to specify a particular group of recipients: the community at large is addressed. No doubt there were divisions within the total community, but in the main Old Testament period it is not easy to identify these in the way that does become possible later, when different religious groups (Pharisees, Sadducees, Essenes, and so on) were often at odds with one another in the different aspects of religious practice.

In this context there is one question to which sociological insights might properly be addressed, though that has not always happened. In what milieu were the traditions of the fathers handed down? It used to be supposed that we should envisage the camp-fire of the nomad group as the natural context, but this attractive picture does not seem to be supported by any relevant evidence. Others have held that the stories of the patriarchs formed the basis for liturgical ceremonies at the places with which they were associated, and that it would therefore be natural to suppose that the observance of festivals at the different sanctuaries would be the context for such transmission.

It may be so; but again we should observe how little supporting evidence there is. It may be better to begin by noting how polished a product is the book of Genesis as it has come down to us, not just in the sense that it is written in an elegant prose style (as it is), but also in the literary subtleties which continue to provide new insights for literary critics right up to our own day. We should perhaps bear in mind, from the sociological angle, that the shaping of ancient traditions had a strongly intellectual content; older stories might be embodied, but they were most probably given their present form as part of a process which was a good deal more sophisticated than has sometimes been supposed.

Considerations of this kind may seem very vague and generalized. Nevertheless they are significant on at least two levels. First, they warn us that no book is entirely context-free; since the Old Testament is part of the Bible many may wish to regard it as 'Word of God', but it is also made up of human words, and the more we know of the circumstances in which those words were spoken or written the better will be our understanding of them. Secondly, we can recognize that the usual criteria of analysis are appropriate for Israel as for any other society. A purely idealistic picture of ancient Israel is not appropriate.

Israel as unique?

But does not such a conclusion contradict an important strand within the Old Testament and its own understanding of Israel? 'Thou art an holy people unto the LORD thy God, and the LORD hath chosen thee to be a peculiar people unto himself, above all the nations that are upon the earth' (Deut. 14: 2). This is the AV translation; RSV has, instead of 'peculiar people', the less vivid but more conventional 'a people for his own possession'. These words are part of the extended sermon put into the mouth of Moses, addressed to a people pictured as being not yet in possession of the land which they believed to be theirs. The apparent context is a time before Israel had ever reached Palestine; this may well be a literary device to bring out the similarity between that situation and the one in which the actual audience found itself: a community in exile, driven out of their ancestral land. But the important point for our immediate concern is that this is a sermon addressed to a group bound together by common religious loyalty; it is not in any normal sense a sociological account of that community.

To a remarkable extent, however, it, and other comparable claims made elsewhere in the Old Testament, have been treated as if they were statements of empirical fact, and as a consequence Israel has been regarded as different in kind from all the other societies of the ancient Near East. It is clear, therefore, that consideration of the nature of Israelite society must involve two levels of enquiry: first, to ask if there is any sense in which we are justified in speaking of the uniqueness of Israel over against its neighbours; secondly, to consider in more detail the social structures and institutions of ancient Israel, as they are reflected in the pages of the Old Testament. Whether in addition it is also useful to attempt to apply some of the distinctive methods and theories of particular sociologists is a much more disputed question, for reasons which will emerge during the course of this chapter.

The first issue, however, concerns the propriety of speaking of ancient Israel as 'unique'. Here, clearly, care in the use of terms is needed. There is a vital sense in which each one of us is unique as an individual; and similarly each larger grouping or community of which we form part is also unique; there is nothing else quite like it. At the other extreme it is clear that there must be valid bases for comparison between Israel and its neighbours. Israel was subject to the same external pressures and natural phenomena as everyone else: war, drought, earthquake, famine. Israel could be included among the lists of nations conquered by Assyrian or Babylonian kings without any suggestion that this particular nation was somehow different in kind from all others. Even if the claim to uniqueness be narrowed to the religious area, it is still the case that when we come to consider the particular religious phenomena which are the special concern of the Old Testament, we find that Israel, like its neighbours, worshipped its God in temples, at regular festivals, with sacrificial rites and religious personnel. Further, the names of many of these religious phenomena are attested much more generally in the ancient Near East. In externals, at least, it soon becomes clear that the area of possible uniqueness must be drastically narrowed down.

These points may seem trivial and obvious, and perhaps they are; yet it is surprising how often they are overlooked. A well-known text-book of the 1950s, by a distinguished Old Testament scholar, the late Professor G. E. Wright, bore the title *The Old Testament against its Environment*. The key word in that title was 'against'. Israel was pictured as in some way set over against its surroundings, as being different, not only in religious perceptions, but also in its very foundations as a society. A familiar example may illustrate the point. In 1 Samuel 8 the demand of the elders to Samuel, 'Appoint for us a king to govern us like all the nations' (v. 5), provokes Samuel's displeasure, and the story goes on to suggest that such a demand is in fact a rejection of their God and of his kingly rule over them. It is not necessary to discuss here the difficult question whether it is likely that the people would have thought of their God in kingly terms before they had ever had experience of an earthly king; the immediately relevant point is that the theological verdict of this chapter has often been treated as if it were a sociological dictum, that Israel was different in kind from all surrounding nations. For other nations kingship was an essential part in their becoming a nation; Israel, on this view, was betraying its own identity by the desire for a king.

What kind of origins?

With another primary source of dispute, however, no easy or agreed solution is possible. This concerns the issue, already alluded to more than once, of Israel's origins. A surface reading of the earlier books of the Old Testament, from Genesis to Joshua, gives the clear impression that Israel began its corporate life in the desert, as a nomadic or semi-nomadic group; that its earliest contacts with settled society were of an antagonistic kind, involving slavery in Egypt; and that it was only through a special divine dispensation that Israel was brought to a settled agricultural existence in Palestine. (Exod. 3: 15–20 provides a brief programmatic summary of the people's history seen in this way.)

Other parts of the Old Testament provide references, scattered but broadly consistent, which appear to support this general picture. In Hosea we twice (12: 9; 13: 4) find this put as a divine assertion

I am the LORD your God
from the land of Egypt;

and the Ten Commandments begin with a very similar phrase
(Exod. 20: 2). But statements of this kind scarcely reflect historical
memories; rather, they represent the viewpoint of the editors and
the religious beliefs of the people at the time they were set down in
their final form. Much the same can be said of those sermonic
passages found in, for example, Hosea 2 and Jeremiah 2, where the
period of wandering in the wilderness before the settlement in the
Promised Land is treated as a kind of honeymoon before the people
were affected by the corrupting influence of Canaanite civilization.
Numerous Psalms (e.g. 78, 105, 106) also recite a similar past
history as a liturgical way of showing how God had guided his
people, rewarding them when they had been loyal, punishing them
at times of disobedience.

But are these religious assertions reasonably accurate statements
of the development of the people which can be supported by
empirical evidence? It is sometimes argued that the story must be
broadly true, in that no people would have invented a story of their
own origin that cast themselves in so unflattering a light as slaves in
a foreign land; but it is not at all clear that this is necessarily so. The
statements we have been considering are religious claims, whose
primary purpose was the glorification of the mighty acts of their
God, and while Israel's own part in the story of the deliverance from
Egypt may have been a modest one, there is no doubt that all forms
of that story portray Yahweh's role as that of a powerful deliverer,
able to overthrow all his enemies. It is in fact striking that, with the
exception of the passages in Hosea 2 and Jeremiah 2 already
alluded to, almost nowhere in the Old Testament is a past time
spent in the wilderness regarded as the ideal period of the people's
history, or the suggestion made that a return to that wilderness
would be an appropriate promise for the future. Instead, it is
Palestine which is the 'land flowing with milk and honey' (Exod. 3:
8 and frequently). Indeed, the basic setting out of the promise to
Abraham centres round the assurance to him of possession of a new
land (Gen. 13: 14–17 and frequently). Though there are difficulties
in taking this as a simple statement of historical fact, there can be no

disputing its theological importance: it lays down a basic pattern which is followed through much of the Old Testament.

It is sometimes argued that there were groups in ancient Israel who retained a kind of 'desert ideal' and resisted the blandishments of urban civilization. Thus, in Jeremiah 35, we find a group known as the Rechabites who claim that they do not touch wine or build houses: 'we have no vineyard or field or seed; but we have lived in tents' (Jer. 35: 9 f.). Clearly this claim pictures the Rechabites as rejecting the ordinary standards and values of society. It remains doubtful, however, whether it represents a kind of nomadic ideal, as is often held. Perhaps they may better be understood as itinerant metalworkers or craftsmen, the kind of group which would inevitably be on the fringe of society.

However this may be, it is clear that for the great majority the theme of a nomadic, wilderness past seems to have played little part in their day-to-day lives. Israel was a settled, mainly agricultural society, with a capital city, an urbanized social structure, and a governmental hierarchy responsible for foreign and diplomatic affairs. Its religious institutions, which are of course of particular concern to the Old Testament, are those of a peasant agricultural society: regular festivals related to the annual round of harvest, fixed places of worship, and an establishment of religious personnel closely comparable to that of other societies.

Like other states in the ancient near East, Israel was governed by a king, and though some attempt is made, notably as we have seen in 1 Samuel 8 and also in Hosea 8: 4, to suggest that kingship was in some way incompatible with Israel's distinctive status, it seems probable that this was a later verdict passed in the light of the disastrous failure of kingship, when Israel had been defeated by its enemies, and its whole future as a nation was in doubt.

Pre-monarchical society

It could, of course, be argued that this settled situation represented a development away from Israel's desert origins, and this is indeed a view which has often been put forward. Thus, the account of the establishment of kingship in 1 Samuel 8 might be regarded as retaining valid ancient insights, even if its final form is from a much later period. In that chapter, to want a king is to be 'like all the nations' (v. 5), with the implication that other surrounding nations had kings, but that Israel had in some way resisted or rejected such a development. Such a viewpoint would characteristically regard the 'judges period' as either implicitly or explicitly a kind of experiment with a form of government distinctive to Israel. Thus, pre-monarchical Israel has sometimes been described as an 'amphictyony', a gathering of tribes around one single central sanctuary, and such a description often carries with it the inference that a unique constitutional experiment was involved. (The word 'amphictyony' comes from Greek meaning 'those who dwell around', i.e. around a particular sanctuary. But there is no suggestion that the institution was borrowed from Greece: the Greek parallel is not more than an interesting basis of comparison.)

In recent years this whole mode of understanding Israel's origins has increasingly come to be questioned. We have noted already that if there was a wilderness or nomadic ideal, it appears to have played little significant role in Israel's day-to-day life as a settled society. It has even come to be questioned how far it is legitimate to seek Israel's origins outside the land of Canaan at all. There is no reference to Israel in any non-biblical text as a group or society living anywhere other than in Canaan. The Hebrew language bears a close similarity to that spoken and written in Canaan, and it is indeed referred to in one passage as 'the language of Canaan' (Isa. 19: 18). There are no traces of distinctively Israelite archaeological remains anywhere other than in Canaan. All the institutions of which we have record seem to be those of a settled agricultural society of the type characteristic of Canaan. Indeed, much socio-anthropological study in recent years has challenged the very idea that there were recurrent waves of 'nomads' or 'semi-nomads' inhabiting the desert but eager to gain a grip on the better agricultural land if opportunity should present itself. In fact it seems that true nomadism only emerged at a somewhat later date with the domestication of the camel.

Building on this, one recent and much discussed presentation of Israel's origins, already referred to in our discussion of historical problems (p. 28 f. above), has argued that they should be seen not in the terms presented by the Bible itself as an invasion or infiltration from outside the land, but rather in terms of a rebellion by an oppressed lower class against its rulers. The Amarna letters, discovered in Egypt late in the nineteenth century, provide a vivid picture of the way in which in the fourteenth century BC various local rulers in Canaan, who were technically in a vassal relation to the Egyptian Pharaoh, were finding it increasingly difficult to maintain law and order; and the argument would run that these difficulties became more acute and were never really resolved. The Amarna letters make frequent reference to a group called the Apiru or Habiru, and it may be that this was a social rather than an ethnic grouping, a class on the fringe of the existing structures of society who continued to pose an increasing threat to those structures. On this view the Old Testament material relating to the pre-monarchical period would, to some extent at least, present similar events from the point of view of the Habiru or Hebrews. Thus, in Judges 4–5, for example, we have the account of the defeat of Sisera, a classic example of the ability of guerrillas to turn local knowledge of the terrain and sudden climatic changes to their own account. If to these local developments was added knowledge of a reverse inflicted upon the Egyptian Pharaoh in his own country (that is, what has come to be called the Exodus tradition) then it becomes possible to posit a picture of a kind of 'peasants' revolt', differing from other so-named movements in that it was ultimately successful.

It should be emphasized that it becomes *possible* to posit such a picture. We have seen already in the discussion of historical problems that our knowledge of the period is inadequate to allow a precisely worked-out reconstruction. For our immediate purpose it is sufficient to note that such a presentation of the emergence of ancient Israel is not shaped by religious idealism, but presents the early development of the society in the kind of terms which could be applied to the study of any society. As such it provides an appropriate transition to our next area of consideration: the actual social structures and institutions of ancient Israel.

The social structure of Israel

Such a transition is also rendered appropriate by the fact that Max Weber, one of the founding fathers of modern sociology, was himself Jewish, and one of his most influential works, *Ancient Judaism*, was concerned with the structure of society in ancient Israel. Indeed, the theory of a pre-monarchical amphictyony, to which reference has been made, was heavily indebted to the sociological insights of Weber. There is a sense, then, in which the Old Testament provided one of the matrices from which serious sociological study developed.

There is, nevertheless, a considerable area of dispute as to the propriety, or even the possibility, of applying modern sociological insights to ancient Israel. Put simply, the problem is that we have no means of knowing how complete or balanced is our picture of ancient Israelite society. For all intents and purposes our knowledge is confined to what may be gleaned from the Old Testament itself. This means, first, that the characteristic controls upon which sociologists rely to assess their evidence against a larger context can never be present. Further, the Old Testament is in no sense a neutral record; it is a body of books pleading on behalf of one particular religious interpretation of events, and as such, it is argued by many scholars, it is too polemical and one-sided to provide a satisfactory working model for sociological study. The picture of ancient Israel which emerges from the Old Testament is of a society overwhelmingly influenced by religious and cultic concerns, and it may well be that this says little about Israel as a society and a great deal about the nature of our evidence.

Cautions of this kind are certainly salutary, but it is doubtful whether they should lead to the complete exclusion of sociological methods of enquiry. In an ancient society, as in a modern one, those methods rely heavily on the unstated assumptions, the implicit rather than the explicit witness of the evidence that has come down to us. It is also relevant to bear in mind that religious interests will in any case be prominent for very many readers and students of the Old Testament. This being so, we may legitimately ask whether, recognizing the need to limit ourselves to the religious structures of society, it is possible to trace any features of those structures which were peculiar to, or at least especially distinctive of, ancient Israel. For an example which has engendered much recent discussion we may consider the role of prophets.

The role of prophets

It will at once be obvious that a good deal of confusion and ambiguity surrounds the terms 'prophet' and 'prophecy'. For a start, these English words derive from Greek, not Hebrew; and in Greek the *prophētēs* was one who could 'speak before'. Sometimes this meant 'speaking before' a divine being in the sense of interpreting his or her words; more often it meant foretelling, predicting what would happen in the future. Much, but not all, common English usage reflects an understanding of this kind. By contrast the Hebrew word for a prophet is *nabi* (plural, *nebiim*), and it is certainly not self-evident that a comparable predictive power was automatically attributed to those who exercised the role of *nabi*.

A second source of confusion arises from the fact that we have already noted, that in the Hebrew Bible a much larger body of material than we should expect is classified as 'the Prophets'. As we saw in chapter 1, this designation includes Joshua, Judges, Samuel, and Kings ('the Former Prophets') as well as the books associated with individual prophetic figures ('the Latter Prophets'). This clearly warns us that, at some stage in the handing down of the sacred traditions, the association of 'being a prophet' had changed: no longer was it associated primarily with a particular class of religious personnel, but rather it had come to be linked with a particular type of religious writing with a message to convey.

Indeed this point has been taken a good deal further by some scholars, who have maintained that the *nabi* was not an especially prominent or important figure in ancient Israel's religious institutions. The reason for the apparent prominence, they would argue, lies in the fact that the book of Deuteronomy issued from prophetic circles; that it regarded words spoken by prophets as *the* way in which God had chosen to reveal his will to his people; and that therefore everything which could be regarded as a true word from God must be regarded as having been uttered by a prophet. So Amos, for example, came to be regarded as a *nabi* even though there is evidence (Amos 7: 14) that in fact he was hostile to the *nebiim* of his day. In a similar way all the great figures of Israel's past—Elijah, Samuel, even Moses himself according to Deuteronomy 18: 15— came to be enlisted in the ranks of the prophets. In their lifetime they had not been *nebiim*, but had carried out a variety of occupations; but because their words had come to be acknowledged as genuinely inspired by God, it was the view of the Deuteronomists that they must have been prophets, for they held that all true guidance from God came through prophets.

Theories of this kind have not won general acceptance for a variety of reasons, though there is very probably an element of truth in them. It is unlikely, for example, that the presentation of Moses as a *nabi* is anything other than an idealization by the author of Deuteronomy. But while we should probably continue to regard the *nebiim* as an important element in Israel's religious structures, we are warned that too precise a degree of sociological analysis should not be anticipated. The material relating to prophets has been shaped in accordance with particular religious presuppositions and ideals.

Despite all this it may still be profitable to examine a little further the question of the precise role of the *nabi* in Israelite society. One immediately striking fact is the apparent lack of any precisely comparable figure in other ancient Near Eastern societies. The other major religious roles in the Old Testament, kings and priests, can easily and clearly be paralleled elsewhere, but when we turn to the *nabi* no such parallel naturally suggests itself. It is, of course, quite easy to find religious functionaries whose role resembled that of the *nabi*. Thus, in the texts from Mari we hear of figures whose function was to give oracles as a means of conveying the divine will to individuals or communities. Others are pictured as pleading with the god on behalf of such individuals or communities. Another common device was the employment of various techniques, usually and perhaps rather confusingly lumped together as 'ecstasy', in order to attune oneself to the divine. (The Egyptian *Tale of Wen-Amun* provides a lively illustration of this.) But these parallels are so broad and general that they could be applied to many different religious systems in many different periods. Again, it may be significant that, as far as present knowledge goes, no other ancient Semitic language has a word cognate with *nabi* to denote a similar functionary. The Old Testament itself, however, appears not to regard the phenomenon of prophetism as something unique to Israel. The story of Elijah, for example, finds no difficulty in

presenting him as being opposed by prophets of Baal and of
Asherah, that is, by *nebiim* who served different gods (1 Kgs. 19: 18,
etc.).

Prophets as royal servants

It may be that a more promising line in trying to 'plot' the role of
prophets in relation to the society of their day is to begin by noting
that all those whom we can plausibly identify as *nebiim* were active
during the monarchical period. Both Abraham (Gen. 20: 7) and
Moses (Deut. 18: 15) are spoken of as prophets, but it is widely
agreed that this is a later reflection upon their importance, and that
it would be quite misleading to envisage either Abraham or Moses
as a *nabi*. Samuel's role is not easy to establish; the stories about
him in 1 Samuel present him sometimes as a prophet, but also as a
judge and a priest; later traditions about him refer to him primarily
as an intercessor (Jer. 15: 1; Ps. 99: 6), and it is very difficult to be
certain which is the most ancient and reliable of the various strands
of tradition relating to him. But we may certainly note that in the
form in which the text has come down to us Samuel is pictured both
as the head of a group of *nebiim* (1 Sam. 19: 20) and as the one who
played a crucial role in the establishment of the monarchy.

From that time on references to prophets become frequent.
David in his campaigns against Saul had with him as part of his
entourage a prophet named Gad (1 Sam. 22: 5), who was still acting
as an intermediary of the divine will to the king at a much later
period (2 Sam. 24: 11–14).

Throughout the monarchical period, there are references to
prophets. The line comes to an effective end with Ezekiel, whose
oracles are dated by the years of the last surviving king of Judah,
Jehoiachin, who was by then, like Ezekiel himself, in exile. (Haggai
and Zechariah were active fifty years later than Ezekiel, but they are
not a real exception to the link between the king and prophets, for
they were concerned with the possibility of the re-establishment of
the Davidic monarchy under Zerubbabel.) There are occasional
references to prophets being active at a later period (e.g. in Neh. 6:
14, where those in question may have been associated with the
governor Sanballat as part of his staff, for in 6: 12 it is said that

Tobiah and Sanballat had 'hired' prophets), and it is almost certainly the case that anonymous additions continued to be made to the collections of prophetic oracles which were handed down from an earlier time (e.g. Isa. 24–7). Stories about prophets from a previous age might continue to be told: the book of Jonah would be the best example of this. Nevertheless a good case can be made for saying that the period of activity of the *nebiim* was for all practical purposes the time of the monarchy.

If this were so, it might then be possible to take the argument a stage further by maintaining that the role of the *nabi* was characteristically in some kind of relation to the royal court, and that prophets were basically paid royal officials, likened by some to a court vizier. Sometimes the entourage would be a large one. I Kings 22: 6 speaks of 'about four hundred men', while the story of the conflict between Elijah and the partisans of Jezebel refers to 'four hundred and fifty prophets of Baal and four hundred prophets of Asherah' (I Kgs. 18: 19). Such numbers may well have been exaggerated in the interests of the story-teller, for in each of these contexts it is the one individual who remains loyal to his God when all the others have fallen away. Nevertheless reference to such large numbers cannot have been wholly unrealistic if the story was to retain any verisimilitude. More generally, the books of Samuel and Kings have many stories which portray the prophets as in some sense royal servants. Occasionally they are seen as obediently doing the will of their royal masters; more frequently we have scenes of conflict, since in the editors' eyes the majority of the kings did 'what was evil in the sight of the LORD'. The encounters of Isaiah with Ahaz (Isa. 7) or of Jeremiah with Zedekiah (Jer. 37) could readily be seen as examples of independent prophets challenging their royal masters.

Thus far a coherent and reasonably plausible picture can be built up. History provides many examples of religious figures who have risen to eminence in royal courts despite their refusal to fall in with all their masters' whims; Thomas à Becket in medieval England is one of the best known. The supposed access of such individuals to the divine no doubt acted as a deterrent to any too drastic punishment. To that extent the king of Israel's words about Micaiah in I Kings 22 are entirely understandable; there is another prophet who has not yet been called, for 'I hate him, for he never prophesies good concerning me but evil' (v. 8)—yet of course he retains his position on the royal staff.

The question still remains, however, whether this model should be regarded as determinative for all the prophets referred to in the Old Testament. What are we to make of those prophets some of whose oracles have been preserved in the books named after them, but of whom we have little or no relevant biographical information? Are they also to be seen as in any sense royal officials? More often, such prophets as Amos and Hosea have been regarded as in opposition to, set over against, the prophets of the royal court. Sometimes, indeed, this opposition has been described in terms that seem to be exaggerated, by describing the court prophets as 'professional' as if that were in some sense a term of abuse. There is in fact no need to raise doubts about the 'professionalism' of any of the prophets; prophetism was regarded as a skilled vocation, demanding the mastery of its particular techniques, and, as with other skilled vocations ever since, from time to time its practitioners would be divided among themselves.

The point however remains that the particular sociological criterion which we have been applying seems not to work well in regard to the eighth-century prophets whose words have been gathered into books. Attempts have therefore been made to discover other ways in which the prophetic office could be placed within the total spectrum of Israelite society, or at least its religious aspects. Two such attempts may be mentioned here by way of illustration.

Different names for prophets

The first of these relates to the different names by which prophets are described in the Old Testament. We have so far made reference only to the word *nabi*, which normally is the Hebrew underlying the 'prophet' of English translations. But at least three other terms are used as descriptive of particular prophets: 'man of God' (a term used especially of Elijah, 1 Kgs. 17: 17–24, and of Elisha, very frequently in 2 Kgs. 4–13, and also on occasion of anonymous figures, as in 1 Kgs. 13); and two different Hebrew words each usually translated as 'seer': *ḥozeh* and *roeh*. The question naturally arises whether these are simply variants used for literary effect, or come from different sources, or whether the role being assigned to the individual differs in accordance with the title by which he is described.

A frequently recurring concern of sociologists has been role theory, that is to say, the significance inherent in the descriptions we give to the particular roles enacted by different groups in a society, and especially the importance of the names by which they are described. In the context of the Christian community, for example, the words 'priest' and 'presbyter', which etymologically are very closely linked, may convey quite different impressions because of the different religious roles associated with those so described. The attempt has therefore been made to link the names given to different religious functionaries in the Old Testament with particular roles, so that to call someone a *nabi* would describe him in a different way from calling him a *ḥozeh* or a *roeh*.

Ingenious though this is, it is very doubtful whether such a proposal can satisfactorily be carried through on the evidence available. Elisha, for example, is described both as a man of God and as a prophet (*nabi*) in the course of the same story (2 Kgs. 6: 10, 13); and much dispute has centred around the interpretation of 1 Samuel 9: 9, which ends with the note 'he who is now called a prophet was formerly called a seer'. In 1 Samuel 9 we may note that the terms 'man of God' and seer (*roeh*) are used, apparently interchangeably, to describe the same individual; and that there is no other evidence which would seem to support the implication of verse 9, that 'prophet' was a later usage than 'seer'. Possible resolutions of these difficulties can be put forward, but enough has perhaps been said to illustrate some of the problems inherent in applying a theory addressed to contemporary societies to a body of literature from a long vanished society.

Central and peripheral prophets

The second application of sociological methods to the study of prophetism makes less precise claims, with both the advantages and the drawbacks that that implies. A characteristic feature both of stories about prophets (e.g. 1 Kgs. 22) and of prophetic oracles (e.g. Jer. 23: 9–40) is the opposition between different prophets that is revealed. A particularly striking illustration of this phenomenon is provided by Jeremiah 28, where Jeremiah and Hananiah are each described as 'the prophet'; each claims to speak in the name of 'the LORD of Hosts, the God of Israel' (vv. 2, 14); each uses symbolic devices ('yoke-bars', of wood and of iron) as a means of authenticating the message he gives (vv. 10–14); yet the message of the two prophets is flatly contradictory (vv. 11, 15). Jeremiah ends by accusing his opponent of deceit and announcing his conviction of Hananiah's imminent death—which did indeed occur, according to a laconic note at the end of the chapter (v. 17).

In this case, as in the story of Micaiah in 1 Kings 22, it was possible to interpret the course of events in such a way as to show very quickly that one prophet was right and another wrong, but there must have been many occasions when so dramatic an outcome did not take place. In such circumstances it is possible to accuse one's opponents of falsehood, and this may sometimes have been justified. If Micah 3: 5–8 is to be taken as an objective description, then it would seem as if Micah's opponents were concerned only with their own selfish interests. But even here these words read more naturally as the attacks of an enemy than as a straightforward recording of objective facts; no doubt if the words of the prophets here condemned had been preserved, we should receive a very different impression.

The attempt has therefore been made to approach confrontations such as these, and other material where very different understandings of the prophetic role are found, from another angle. Instead of value judgements on truth and error, or sincerity and deception, perhaps a different assessment of the prophetic role would be helpful. Such an assessment has been proposed in seeing the prophets as either 'central' or 'peripheral'.

These terms have been frequently used in the sociology of religion to describe two rather different roles played by religious figures comparable to prophets. In many contexts religion occupies an ambiguous role in relation to a society. On the one hand it may be regarded as a prop, supporting and legitimating the norms and values of the society, and expressing that support in terms of divine approval for the actions of the community. On the other hand it may function as a critique, challenging the moral and political bases of the society's structure, using its religious authority to call into question what are taken to be the complacent assumptions of the community and its leaders that they are acceptable before God. Individuals who function in the first sense may be spoken of as central; those in the second group can be called peripheral. The terms are descriptive; 'peripheral' is not here used, as it sometimes is in other contexts, in a dismissive sense to mean 'of little importance'.

It will be readily apparent that some at least of the confrontations between different prophets can helpfully be seen in such terms as this. In Jeremiah 28, for example, the optimistic assumptions of Hananiah, that God must be pleased with the worship of his community, and that any mishap is no more than a passing affliction, are entirely characteristic of the central figure, while the bitter accusations of Jeremiah are equally those associated with the peripheral figure, excluded from and opposed to the religious assumptions and the decision-making process of his time. Equally revealing is the picture of the royal entourage in 1 Kings 22; the 400 prophets (v. 6) are the central figures, whose enquiry of God can be guaranteed to produce an answer corresponding with the king's own wishes, whereas Micaiah is a classic peripheral figure, of whom, as we have already observed, the king says, 'I hate him, for he never prophesies good concerning me, but evil' (v. 8). The fact that Micaiah is nevertheless retained on the royal staff would now be understood in terms slightly different from those used when we first considered this passage (above, p. 69). It is easy to see that it was politic to keep so potentially dangerous a figure in close contact; at the same time this raises questions (which are also applicable with Jeremiah) concerning the extent to which someone so closely involved with affairs can legitimately be described as peripheral.

Other difficulties in the application of this kind of sociological analysis arise when we apply it to the different prophetic books. Thus, it could be argued that the eighth-century prophets, Amos, Hosea, and Micah, all of whose oracles contain fierce attacks upon the establishment of their day and in particular upon contemporary religious practice, were characteristic peripheral figures; and that

Haggai and Zechariah, active at a time when the Jerusalem community was just re-establishing itself after the trauma of the exile, were central figures, whose role was to help in setting up the religious bases of the Jerusalem group as a loyal part of the Persian empire.

In each case an interpretation along these lines may indeed be right, but at least two limitations relating to such sociological applications should be noted. The first is simple: it is to ask how far theories of this kind actually increase our knowledge. It is clear from even the most superficial reading of the eighth-century prophets that they were opposed to much of the religious and social practice of their day; and sociological labelling may not increase our awareness of this phenomenon.

More important, however, is the second limitation. The type of sociological approach to which we have been referring is concerned with prophets as individuals, figures carrying out a particular religious role in the context of the society of their day. In fact it is not at all clear that we can have significant access to the prophets of the Old Testament as individual religious figures. In most cases all the information we have comes from the books named after them. There is no agreement as to which parts of those books are the original utterances of the prophet after whom they are named, or what kind of editorial and redactional shaping they have undergone. In particular, individual oracles are now context-free, with little indication of the circumstances in which they were first delivered. Thus, we should need to ask how far the denunciations of religious practice found in Amos, for example, owe their present form to the awareness of a later editor that those religious practices had come to an end with the overthrow of the northern kingdom by an enemy power. Indeed, the very fact that the words of prophets were handed down at all suggests that they were envisaged as being relevant and applicable to all kinds of different historical situations. By contrast, any biographical interest in the original prophetic figures is minimal. We are reminded that the Old Testament is literature, and that a sociological approach to the figures mentioned in it is fraught with difficulty.

Sociology and literature

Insights from sociology can, however, be applied to literature as well as to individuals. The Old Testament as we have it is a collection of literature gathered and edited in Jerusalem; the fate of that city was therefore of crucial importance. Considerable insights can be gained from observing the different reactions to the fate of Jerusalem and its rulers at a time when that fate differed so dramatically from the expectations of the religious community in its liturgy.

The sociological theory known as 'cognitive dissonance' is revealing at this point. It is concerned with the ways in which individuals and groups react, both in their own lives and in their literature, to apparently irreconcilable conflicts between their expectations and the reality with which they find themselves confronted. The fall of Jerusalem in 587 BC provides a classic example of such a situation. Many Psalms had proclaimed complete confidence that Jerusalem was inviolable; it was,

> the city of our God,
> which God establishes for ever.   (Ps. 48: 8)

Similarly its king had been assured of Yahweh's continuing protection, so that all enemies would be overthrown:

> You are my son,
> today I have begotten you.
> Ask of me, and I will make the nations your heritage,
> and the ends of the earth your possession.   (Ps. 2:7)

The reality was sharply at odds with these confident proclamations. The city was captured in 597 and its king exiled; when those who remained confident in the applicability of the divine promises to their contemporary situation raised a revolt against the Babylonians the city was destroyed and the remaining pretensions of the Davidic line ended.

How could such a development, so sharply at odds with the deepest expectations of the religious community, be explained? At the individual and personal level, as we have seen, there is insufficient evidence for any conclusions to be reached. But the literary reactions are revealing. In some passages we can see the attitudes which might be expected in such a situation in any people's history: bitterness against the enemy, and especially those thought to have taken unfair advantage of Jerusalem's plight, as in the harsh cries against Babylon and the Edomites in Psalm 137: 7–9 and in other texts from the period such as Obadiah and Jeremiah 50–1. Elsewhere the dominant note is one of lament for the departure of past glories, as in the book of Lamentations. Reactions such as these are so universal that they need no particular sociological insight to explain them. No doubt, too, there were those who abandoned belief in the effective power of their own God and supposed that the Babylonian deities were much superior to him. Of this attitude we have no direct evidence in the Old Testament, though the condemnations in Isaiah 40–8 may reflect such a development.

More revealing for our present purpose, however, is the way in which an attempt is made to come to terms with the disaster in a way which preserved belief in the power and effectiveness of Israel's own God. The classic example of this is to be found in Joshua–2 Kings, the collection of books often referred to as the Deutero-nomistic history. Here a selection of traditions from the people's past history is set out in terms which show how it was their own failure to observe the known commandments of God which had brought about their present plight. A series of 'sermons' (e.g. Judg. 2: 6–end; 2 Kgs. 17: 6–end) is designed to show the inevitable consequences of the people's behaviour; the establishment of kingship is shown to pose problems for the ultimate sovereignty of Yahweh as supreme king (1 Sam. 8); yet not all is lost—hope for the future may still be maintained, as is shown by the reference in 1 Kings 8: 46–53 to the efficacy of prayers even in exile.

It is obviously possible to regard these different reactions to disaster from a variety of standpoints. The particular contribution of sociology at this point may be no more than illustrative, but is not the less valuable for that. One of the characteristics of sociological study has been to set up models of human behaviour in given sets of circumstances, and here the way in which the writings of the Old Testament developed through greatly changed circumstances is particularly revealing. No less important at the literary level is the fact that earlier writings which set out a different understanding (such as the Psalms from which we have quoted) were not 'suppressed', but were reinterpreted in the light of changing circumstances.

A religious overview

At this point, however, it is important to notice a considerable limitation of the applicability of sociology to Old Testament study. The Old Testament is a collection of religious texts; indeed we are sometimes liable to think that religion was the only matter of concern in ancient Israel. The important point in the present context is that all the explanations offered of different developments in the people's history are religious explanations; social, economic, and political issues are mentioned only in so far as they affect religious concerns. This means that the picture that is drawn must inevitably be a partial one; for much of the people's life our knowledge is too fragmentary to reach confident conclusions. Some would conclude from this that the Old Testament does not provide acceptable material for the sociologist at all; everyone would agree that more than usual care is needed in the application of sociological methods to a body of material for which no independent controls are available.

Cultural awareness

There is, nevertheless, one other way in which sociological awareness has affected our understanding of the Bible, with wide-ranging implications. For centuries many church-people regarded the norms and commands laid down by the biblical text to be determinative for virtually every aspect of human life. Such an attitude is certainly not extinct, but is much less common than it was, at least in matters that would be widely regarded as of peripheral importance in religious observance. Perhaps the most familiar example comes from the New Testament, where Paul's injunction that women should not pray or prophesy with their head uncovered (1 Cor. 11: 3–15) has been interpreted as implying that women should wear hats in church, a matter of controversy as recently as the Second World War, and still expected in many traditionalist Churches.

One of the reasons advanced for following the biblical require-ment (as it was thought to be) was that if loyalty to the Bible was abandoned in a relatively trivial matter, there was no logical reason why it should not also be given up in much more basic and fundamental points; and here it can readily be seen that a sociological approach might soon be at odds with a more traditional mode of understanding. There are wide areas where the Old Testament in particular appears to lay down very specific laws affecting the life of the family or of the larger community. Are these to be followed literally, or are they to be seen as the particular situation of a particular type of society, which can offer insights and parallels but not binding rules for a twentieth-century society?

One or two examples may serve to illustrate the point. There can be no doubt that the death penalty was laid down in ancient Israel for certain offences: murder, abduction, various sexual offences, and so on (Exod. 21: 12–17; Lev. 20: 1–17). As in other societies, the death penalty does not always seem to have been imposed in practice for those guilty of such offences; there is no suggestion, for example, that Cain should have been killed for the murder of his brother Abel (Gen. 4). But equally it seems clear that capital punishment was a genuine possibility, and it is possible and appropriate to compare Israel's law codes with those of other ancient Near Eastern societies, with which they had much in common. (The famous 'Code' of Hammurabi, king of Babylon, is the best-known, though not always the closest, such example.) It is much less clear that a direct transference can be made from ancient Israel to a twentieth-century context, so as to argue, for example, that a modern state should embody capital punishment within its legislative structure because it is laid down in the Bible.

What applies to criminal law has a potentially much wider field of reference. The existence of slaves; the royal harem; the possibility of polygamy—all of these are taken for granted in the Old Testament, with no suggestion that their very existence was a matter for condemnation. Once again custom in Israel can legitimately be compared with what is known of neighbouring countries, and sociological comments made on the similarities and the differences that are thus revealed; it seems unlikely that even the most literal follower of biblical ways would regard these as areas for adoption in a modern society.

One other comment needs to be made in this theme. We are warned of the dangers of 'reading off' the biblical patterns of social and family life and ethics and attempting to apply them to present-day circumstances because those patterns were governed by the social circumstances of their time. We must equally not forget that we are in our turn governed by the particular circumstances and expectations generated by our own society. We are no more immune from changing social structures than were the biblical writers.

By way of conclusion, one other insight of the sociologist may be noted. Many stories are told, most of them no doubt apocryphal, of encounters with sociologists who proved to have more interest in the student than in the object of study. One of the most characteristic sociological insights, in Old Testament study as elsewhere, has been its ability to comment upon the assumptions and methods of study traditionally associated with the discipline. Thus, when the prophets are studied from within a Christian Church context, they are regarded as religious figures pointing the way forward to a greater religious figure who is to come after them: Jesus Christ. Their message, that is to say, is brought into harmony with the appropriate religious context. When they are studied by university teachers working alongside colleagues in other academic disciplines, then it is much more likely that they will be viewed through the literary, or historical, or philosophical spectacles that are deemed to be appropriate in that academic context. When they are read in a Third World context, then they are seen as pointing the way to liberation from the pressures of an unjust society, as corrupt today as were the political and religious leaders of Israel nearly 3,000 years ago. The sociologist is notoriously reluctant to say of any two methods of approach to a problem that one is right and another wrong, and so it is here; it remains valid and important to recognize that the sociology of the student is as important as that of what is being studied.

It will be apparent that the emphasis in all of this is very strongly human. It may be an interesting matter of observation that religious practice, or belief in God, plays such and such a part in a society's structures, but it is not in itself determinative; it can only be one subject for study alongside others. In due course we shall need to return to the God-ward, theological, side, but in the mean time there is more that must concern us on the human, anthropological, side.

6

What is Man?

'The proper study of mankind is man.' So wrote Pope, some 250 years ago. His choice of words would be criticized nowadays as sexually stereotyped, but apart from that it might not appear that his aphorism was true when applied to the Bible, which is, after all, a book about God and his relations with humanity. Yet (if not quite in the sense envisaged by Pope) recent biblical studies have been much enriched by the work of anthropologists, whose contributions have brought a different perspective to bear upon the biblical text over against that which has been dominated by historical concerns.

It is important first of all to attempt to remove a likely source of confusion. In the 1970s two books were published whose titles were very similar, but whose contents were quite different. They were *Anthropology of the Old Testament* (by H. W. Wolff; 1974) and *Anthropology and the Old Testament* (by J. W. Rogerson; 1978). The first is essentially the converse of the various theologies of the Old Testament which have been published. They try to draw out the essential features of the Old Testament's view of God; Professor Wolff's book essays a comparable task in showing what the Old Testament has to say about humanity. The Rogerson volume, by contrast, is concerned with the relation between study of the Old Testament and the work of anthropologists; and it is this latter subject which will exercise us in this chapter.

Survivals

The word *anthrōpos* is Greek for 'man', 'mankind' in the generic sense rather than the individual male human being, and so in theory anthropology is that science which is concerned with mankind in all its characteristics and activities. In practice, however, its scope has been more limited than this, and the term is normally used to describe detailed study of the customs and cultures of other societies of the kind which has been widely practised in the Western world during the last two centuries. In particular during the latter part of the nineteenth century and the period up to the Second World War, a great deal of anthropological research was carried out by students from Europe and the United States who went to live among non-Western societies, observing their manner of life in all its aspects. At the more formal level this would involve the study of legal, political, and religious institutions; more spontaneously, living in a society for an extended period gave the observer the opportunity to participate in the less formalized aspects of family and social life, and so to build up a complete picture of a life-style very different in some cases from that of the West. To some extent research of this kind has continued in more recent decades, but it has become much more difficult, partly because of political difficulties, partly because the increasing influence of Western modes of thought has made it much more difficult to find appropriate non-Westernized societies for study. Very often, these reasons have reinforced one another; newly independent countries in, for example, sub-Saharan Africa have been naturally sensitive to any suggestion from the West that they still harbour 'primitives' when their own freshly established governments are anxious to prove how 'up-to-date' they are. It may be expected, therefore, that the scope for this mainly descriptive mode of anthropological investigation will steadily diminish.

It is, however, work of this kind which has provided one of the bases for the contribution of anthropology to our understanding of the Old Testament. It is a common experience today for the visitor to the Holy Land to feel in an instinctive and quite imprecise way that the Arabs, with their traditional clothing and their cautious approach to Western technology, somehow embody its distinctiveness much more than do the Israelis, who are more obviously and directly linked to the twentieth-century West. This instinctive reaction has been reflected in a more precise and scholarly way, by a series of studies which have sought for parallels to biblical customs and practices among the surviving customs and practices of pre-industrial Middle Eastern societies. A classic work in this genre was Robertson Smith's *Lectures on the Religion of the Semites*, first published in 1889. The term 'comparative religion' has been widely and often misleadingly used, but this work, though now a century old, still provides instructive reading and an example of the proper use of a comparative method.

Just one example may be offered of the kind of insight which Robertson Smith's work afforded. A basic assumption running throughout much of the Old Testament is of the importance of a sacrificial cult for the maintenance of proper relations between God and people. It is pictured as going back to the time of the flood, for Noah's first act after his safe deliverance is said to have been that he 'built an altar to the LORD, and took of every clean animal and of every clean bird, and offered burnt offerings' (Gen. 8: 19). Large parts of Exodus, Leviticus, and Numbers are devoted to spelling out the precisely laid down requirements for the proper offering of sacrifice. There are numerous prophetic texts which condemn sacrifice in the way it was being carried out, but it seems clear that this was not a condemnation of sacrifice as such, but a warning of the folly of the community performing such important rites without ensuring that its whole individual and corporate life fitted it to do so properly. (Hos. 6: 6; Mic. 6: 6–8; Isa. 1: 10–17 are among the best known of these texts, which we shall look at again in ch. 9.) Sacrificial offerings, that is to say, were an integral part of the religious life of the Old Testament community.

It would be impossible to find a close parallel to this in any modern society. Ancient Israel was what could now fairly be called a subsistence economy, with famine and drought a real and recurring threat, yet it appears as if the lavish provision of sacrifices retained a very high priority. The prophetic condemnations which have been referred to do not include any suggestion that the community was trying to avoid its responsibilities in this matter; on the contrary, the community was only too ready to suppose that frequent and generous offering of sacrifices ensured the favour of God (Amos 4: 4 f.). (Only one passage, Mal. 1: 8, seems to imply an attempt to avoid the responsibility of offering the best to God.) All of this implies a world very far removed from our own; for a start it is difficult for many to conceive of religious duties being taken with such extreme seriousness, and where religious obligations are important they are nowadays normally envisaged in a much more symbolic or 'spiritual' way.

Comparative methods

To obtain some kind of insight into a society in which sacrifice played so important a part, therefore, it was necessary to consider whether any survivals might still be traced whose life-style was comparable to that of ancient Israel. Such writers as Robertson Smith were able to draw together in their work on the one hand insights from surviving groups of this kind and on the other literary and inscriptional evidence from the ancient world to throw light on Old Testament practice. In other words, a *comparative* method was introduced; practices and texts from widely differing sources were compared for the light that they might shed on the biblical text.

The kind of insights gained from this type of study are clear enough, but before we go further it may be relevant to make certain comments on its implicit limitations. They relate in particular to the problems posed by comparisons. First, in any field of study, comparisons can only be valid if the two subjects being compared are genuinely similar. But it is obvious that this is not the case here: the Old Testament is a body of texts, the end-product of a period of long reflection and elaboration, often with a particular editorial viewpoint imposed upon them; modern primitive 'survivals' are likely to be pre-literate, and in any case the religious practices and customs being surveyed will be viewed through Western and therefore alien eyes. Secondly, valid comparisons are liable to be vitiated if only a small part of the total picture is used. Many cultures have stories which could in a broad sense be regarded as parallel to those which tell of creation and 'the fall' in Gen. 1–3. But there is great danger of the picture being distorted if isolated incidents from different stories are used as the basis for comparison. (This is one of the great limitations of the massive collections by Sir James Frazer, *The Golden Bough* and *Folk Lore in the Old Testament*; the bases for comparison are chosen in a very arbitrary way, and not always even related to the Old Testament text in its existing form but to some putative original which it is claimed can be detected behind the present form of the text.)

The comments made so far are almost of the nature of truisms, which would not be widely disputed. Much more contentious is the problem posed by a third area of questioning in regard to comparative studies. It arises from the fact that comparisons are rarely made in and for themselves; they are normally part of some larger theory concerning the nature of religion or its development, or, even more all-embracingly, concerning mankind as a whole. Is it proper, for example, to speak of mankind as having developed or evolved from more primitive origins, traces of which might be detected in out-of-the way societies little affected by the onward march of progress? More specifically, have religious practice and belief undergone some similar form of evolution to that which can be detected in the biological field? This whole area is one in which no agreement is in sight, and it is therefore not surprising that the anthropological approach is one that continues to arouse great controversy.

The type of anthropology that has so far been referred to is in effect ethnology: the comparison of rites and practices as they are found in different societies. As has been seen, certain areas of dispute arise within it. But there are two other developments within anthropological practice which are of major importance for Old Testament study, and they must now claim our attention.

Tabu

The first may best be illustrated by further consideration of the matter of the sacrificial cultus. This is probably the area of Israelite religious practice which is more alien to the modern Western mind than any other. In the book of Leviticus its requirements are set out in detail, along with other indications of the way in which the purity and holiness of the community before its God are to be maintained. Such a text clearly cannot simply be regarded as a handbook, a reference work for those with the responsibility of carrying out rites of sacrifice and purification, though that may have been part of its function. Rather, it is important to recognize that we are here in an area of life where purely rational means of enquiry and explanation are inadequate; we are involved with what might be dismissed as superstition, but can more appropriately be described as tabu.

This notion is an important one, and needs spelling out for a better understanding of this aspect of the Old Testament. In any community, be it a family or a larger grouping, there will be rites and ceremonies which are of particular importance in laying down the structures within which that community's life is carried on. In all societies, it would appear, there are certain modes of behaviour, certain social conventions, which are observed not on any rational grounds, but as part of some more deep-seated conviction about what is right and acceptable. Religious practice and convention are particularly susceptible to these convictions, and reform or change in religious matters, even in the modern West, often arouses controversy which goes far beyond what might rationally be expected. (An obvious current example would be the dispute in various Christian Churches concerning whether or not women should be admitted to the ministry or priesthood; it is clear that for some the animosity which this proposal arouses can only be likened to a breach of the requirements of tabu.)

A directly biblical example which poses a problem for modern translations relates to the Hebrew word *tsara'ath*, conventionally translated 'leprosy'. Medical research has made it clear that this cannot be an accurate rendering; the symptoms described in the biblical texts are not those of true leprosy ('Hansen's Disease'), and it is most unlikely that leprosy was established in Palestine in the Old Testament period. What is there described must be some form of malignant or at least offensive skin condition such as scabies or an acute form of eczema. But for the modern translator this poses a problem; the words 'leper' and 'leprosy' have a sense beyond the clinical and rational, as descriptive of a condition deeply offensive to other human beings which needs the power of God to put it right. Thus in the New Testament when the effects of Jesus' work are described, the RSV, following the traditional rendering, translates '. . . lepers are cleansed and the deaf hear, and the dead are raised up' (Matt. 11: 5). By comparison GNB's rendering of the first phrase is 'Those who suffer from dreaded skin-diseases are made clean'. Here not only is the rhythm of the traditional version lost but also the effect of the translation is to picture Jesus' work in terms of a medical mission. The threat to ordered human existence implicit in the word 'lepers' is totally lost.

This word can be taken further by considering the use of the word *tsara 'ath* in its Old Testament context. In Leviticus 13–14 the word is used to describe a contagious human ailment, but is also used of conditions which may affect clothing (13: 47–59) or houses (14: 33–53). All together are described as 'the law for leprosy' (14: 57). It would be possible to dismiss such ideas as ignorant superstition, or as illustrative of confusion, a failure to differentiate quite dissimilar problems, and many commentators *have* dismissed these chapters along these lines. But this would seem to be a counsel of despair. The book of Leviticus was almost certainly one of the latest parts of the Pentateuch to reach its final form, and came from that priestly group which was responsible for some of the most profound and ordered texts such as the story of creation in Genesis 1. Why should they have lapsed into basic confusion and misunderstanding here?

It has sometimes been argued that these and other prohibitions in Leviticus, particularly those in chapter 11 relating to clean and unclean animals, are illustrative of a primitive awareness of and concern for hygiene, but neither the reasons stated in Leviticus itself nor the results of modern medical research would lend any particular support to this theory. A more promising manner of approaching these texts has been set out by anthropologists, with particular emphasis on such themes as that of tabu. There were certain states and conditions which introduced pollution into a society, and it was essential for the proper maintenance of that society that pollution should be kept at bay. Hence the elaborate requirements laid down in Leviticus 13–14 to ensure that the 'leprosy' does not spread; the danger which it represents must be kept within bounds.

In the light of considerations such as these it is now possible to look afresh at the place of sacrifice. First, it is surely no accident that the detailed spelling out of the requirements of sacrifice is found in the opening chapters of Leviticus, immediately preceding the chapters we have been discussing. They are closely linked in the overall concern for the upholding of the society before its God. Secondly, the threat of pollution is one which affects a society at its very basis, in its relations with the divine. The sacrificial system was developed, particularly in the later Old Testament period, into an elaborate rationale for maintaining relations between Israel and its God in a state which would keep pollution at bay. And so the precise spelling out of the ritual of sacrifice becomes in a sense almost more important than the sacrifice itself. (This point can perhaps best be illustrated from the Mishnah, the post-biblical collection of material expounding the Torah. Though it was compiled at least a century after the destruction of the temple by the Romans in AD 70 and the cessation of the sacrificial system, it still spells out in elaborate and intricate detail the minutiae of the sacrificial offerings; the profound concern for the proper maintenance of society which we have noted remained even when it was no longer possible to carry out the appropriate rituals.)

Holiness

A third point with regard to the understanding of sacrifice concerns the matter of holiness. We have been looking in this chapter mainly at the book of Leviticus, and it is no coincidence that the word 'holy' occurs in Leviticus and in the closely connected final section of the immediately preceding book, Exodus 28–40, more frequently than anywhere else in the Old Testament. In modern English 'holy' has mainly religious or moral meanings; the first two definitions in the *Concise Oxford Dictionary*, for example, are 'consecrated, sacred' and 'morally and spiritually perfect'. Neither of these is appropriate to bring out the sense of the Hebrew word. That has two aspects, each of which needs to be kept in mind when we approach Exodus and Leviticus. One is the sense of being set apart, something integral to the divine realm. Thus whatever may be consumed of the sacrifices is to be eaten in a holy place, and anyone who touches any part of the offerings becomes holy, that is, himself set apart (Lev. 6: 16, 18). The other aspect of the meaning of the word is the sense of right order, appropriateness, something which is important in all aspects of life, but never more so than in things which pertain to God.

It is not unusual in Leviticus to find these two meanings inherent in one usage. Thus, for example, the classification of clean and unclean animals in Leviticus 11 ends with the repeated 'Be holy, for I am holy' (vv. 44–5). In the context this is clearly not an exhortation to a particular life-style; rather it reminds the community of the fact that they are set apart for God's service, and that the detailed ordering of what is permissible for food and what must be rejected as unclean provides an important example of holiness in the sense of right order in one of the most important aspects of any group's life—what it eats.

There is a particular way in which this understanding of holiness as the maintenance of right order is illustrated by the texts relating to sacrifice. The modern reader of Leviticus, and of other Old Testament texts, is often struck by the fact that the sins or offences which are to be expiated by sacrifice seem not to involve wrongdoing in any discernible sense. No intentional act of trespass appears to be involved. Indeed, in Leviticus 4: 2 we find an expression, 'If anyone sins unwittingly', which would be a contradiction in terms to modern Western thought, for which 'sin' is by definition not something done unwittingly. Thus, sacrificial rituals are prescribed for those who have experienced a bodily discharge, including women in their menstrual periods (Lev. 15); for women who have given birth to a child (Lev. 12); and for those who have had any kind of contact with a dead body (Num. 19). In a comparable way Job is commended for offering sacrifices in case any of his sons had committed sins (Job 1: 5), and such an action is clearly at odds with any kind of theological explanation, which would expect that those who had committed the sin would be those who made the offerings to atone for them. In all these cases what was regarded as the proper or normal state of affairs was at risk, and so sacrifice could be regarded as the appropriate means of restoring a true relation between God and his people. In this, rather than any moral or religious sense, sin and holiness could be regarded as opposed to one another.

This concern for holiness permeates even more of the book of Leviticus, and affects virtually every aspect of the community's life. Because the principles of what constitutes holiness are so very different from those to which we are accustomed, we find some unexpected topics being raised. Leviticus 18, for example, provides the basis for the spelling out of degrees of kindred and affinity within which marriage is forbidden by many modern Western societies, but this was not the original purpose of such commands; rather, the 'wickedness' and 'perversion' which is implicit in breach of these commands lay in the fact that they derogated from the proper structuring of the community, its order before God, in other words, its holiness.

Our last example can be taken from the following chapter, Leviticus 19, with its very unexpected juxtapositions within the same concern for holiness. Thus we find on the one hand regulations concerning how the hair was to be cut (v. 27), on the other the command quoted by Jesus as the second great command in the Law (Mark 12: 31): 'you shall love your neighbour as yourself' (v. 18). Each requirement was in its different way constitutive of the holiness of the community; the prohibition concerning the hair was aimed at those involved in pagan mourning-rites, which were incompatible with the standing of the true community before God, while the command to love the neighbour was not, as it has later been understood, of universal application: the 'neighbour' was the fellow-member of the community, within which harmonious relations were an essential prerequisite of holiness.

Structuralism

The particular insights from anthropology which we have so far considered have not been incompatible with a mainly historical approach to the study of the Old Testament. They could be regarded as complementary to it, particularly in view of the fact that our examples have come mainly from Leviticus. This book is on any showing scarcely susceptible to a historical approach, in the sense that it could be claimed to represent Israelite religious practice of any one identifiable period of history. But other types of anthropological study have been much less consonant with this historical approach, and they constitute the second type of development to which reference was earlier made.

The word 'structure' has several times been used in the preceding pages: an innocent-seeming word, which has in fact given rise to acute and even bitter controversy.

Here reference must be made to a scholar who has not in fact written anything directly relating to the Old Testament, but whose influence in the area we are now considering has been fundamental: the French social anthropologist Claude Lévi-Strauss. He was critical of the kind of ethnological studies which we considered at the beginning of this chapter, maintaining that they were able only to supply a great deal more miscellaneous information without any underlying principle of order or structure by which it could be arranged. The data need to be organized; and the particular clue on to which Lévi-Strauss fastened in order to provide such organization was the idea of basic binary oppositions. Many have become familiar with the binary principle through the application of computer programs, in which each step is taken in accordance with a specific command: do either *this* or *that*. Lévi-Strauss and his followers have maintained that this binary method is not simply a learned skill but the reflection of something basic in the human psyche. The titles of some of Lévi-Strauss's works such as *Le cru et le cuit* (*The raw and the cooked*) illustrate this conviction and hint at a more basic nature–culture antithesis. It will be seen immediately that some of the points already made concerning holiness and its absence (there is no single convenient word to express 'lack of holiness') fit this pattern of expression.

In such a context as this one can see the importance of the idea of 'rites of passage'—a perhaps too literal rendering of the French original *rites de passage*, an expression used to denote those important points in the life of an individual or a community at which fundamental change of status took place. An obvious example relevant to both the biblical and the modern world would be marriage, where the explanatory comment in Genesis 2: 24, 'therefore a man leaves his father and his mother and cleaves to his wife', describes a 'passage' from one set of family structures to another, a practice which is still widely maintained. Religious ceremonies such as confirmation or bar mitzvah would be other examples, and the whole concept is applied by many anthropologists on a more extensive scale.

To take an Old Testament example, one could consider the story of Jacob's encounter with an unnamed adversary at the River Jabbok in Genesis 32. The concept can legitimately be applied at several levels. The whole episode takes place within the larger context of the recipient of the patriarchal blessing of Isaac: will it be Esau, the first-born, or Jacob? The more immediate context is Jacob's marriage, to Leah and Rachel, and the Laban–Jacob antithesis in which this resulted. Within the story itself we see the passage of the Jabbok, which needed to be forded to gain entry into the Promised Land; the human–divine encounter symbolized by the wrestling, for, though Jacob's adversary is only called 'a man' (vv. 24 f.), Jacob recognizes the presence of the divine: 'I have seen God face to face' (v. 30). Important also is the giving of a new name, another important characteristic of many rites of passage (baptism; the woman in marriage usually changes her name; a bishop when enthroned takes on the name of his see). Here Jacob is told that his name will henceforth be Israel (v. 28), which both emphasizes his close links with God and marks him as the eponymous father of the later community of Israel. In the light of such features of the story as these, the introductory comments that Jacob was parted from 'everything that he had and . . . was left alone' (vv. 23 f.) assume a deeper significance; Jacob is stripped of all the features of his previous life as appropriate preparation for the rite he is about to undergo.

This was not Jacob's first mysterious encounter with the divine. On his journey away from his father and mother and from the land of promise he had had a dream which had led him to realize that the place where he was sleeping was Beth-el, which means 'the house of God' (Gen. 28: 10–22). It would be possible to set out in tabular form the various stages of this whole elaborate rite of separation and rejoining, of division and unity, as giving a discernible structure to the whole Jacob episode. For the moment, however, just two points may be relevant. The first is that an approach of this kind raises questions and offers insights quite different from those of more traditional historical enquiry or source-criticism. Stories of this kind are context-free in any historical sense; they are not related to any identifiable historical period. Source-critical analysis of these stories has been a regular feature of commentaries on Genesis, but, whatever earlier sources may have been used, the story in its present form has surely been drawn together to set out some of the polarities which have been mentioned. Secondly, the question is bound to arise whether the insights gained by this kind of approach are not as much literary as anthropological, a tribute to the story-teller's art rather than an illustration of the customs of particular social groups.

The rules of language

This raises one of the most basic and controversial issues in the application of anthropological insights to Old Testament study. It would not be an exaggeration to say that the Lévi-Straussian programme has been an attempt to come to terms with the fundamental workings of the human mind. A potential key to a deeper understanding of those workings arises from the fact of language, the basic need of human beings to communicate with one another. The signs of which all languages are composed are by themselves meaningless and arbitrary, but certain conventions and structures are imposed upon them to enable communication to take place. Anthropologists readily acknowledge their debt to the work done by linguists; what they had perceived in relation to the nature of communication could be applied more generally in the study of mankind. Just as there are grammatical rules which are essential if meaningful communication is to take place, so there are 'rules', conventions, which govern the structures of society, and these can be set out in regular tabular form.

An example which is readily applicable to the Old Testament centres around the use of the term 'myth'. This is one of those words which can cause great confusion owing to the varied senses in which it is used. In everyday language to call something a myth is to call it fiction, often with the sense of fiction masquerading as historical truth. Or the word may be used to describe pre-scientific modes of thought; the controversy over 'de-mythologizing' the Gospels which exercised New Testament scholars in the 1950s and 1960s centred on this kind of understanding. Again, the expression 'myth and ritual' is sometimes found, wherein the myth is the story accompanying and giving sense to what is acted out in a religious ritual. None of these usages quite corresponds to the more general way in which the term is used by anthropologists, though the last is not unrelated. In the 1920s Bronislaw Malinowski wrote extensively

about myth, and in his understanding myth was both a story told
and the underlying reality which it expressed. In this sense the
whole of the Bible can be regarded as myth; it is for Jews or for
Christians the story which underpins their perception of the reality
of their world.

One important implication of this kind of understanding is that it
will be markedly lacking in the kind of historical concerns which
have so dominated biblical study during the period since the Middle
Ages. Both the Bible as a whole and the individual elements which
comprise it are studied as stories, or as part of the one larger story,
without any judgement concerning (or even sometimes any interest
in) a possible historical or geographical basis. Individuals (Cain and
Abel, Abraham and Lot, Saul and David); points of the compass
(North and South); geographical areas (the holy land and the
wilderness; Jerusalem and Damascus): all these, and comparable
examples which could be quoted, are taken as expressing binary
oppositions symbolic of particular realities and have no discernible
empirical basis. Such a method of approach may certainly offer
insights into stories that cannot be seen by more conventional
methods of study; it will often be regarded with suspicion by those
for whom a historical approach is normative, both because it ignores
the historical issues which have so commonly been regarded as
crucial, and because it freely acknowledges that no criteria of proof
are available. Whereas historical assertions can in principle be
falsified—Joshua either did or did not capture Jericho—the
insights of structural anthropology are more like invitations to read
a story in a particular way. It is clear that the tension arises in its
most acute form with regard to narratives; with poetry it would be
generally agreed that historical issues are likely to be much less
prominent.

It may be instructive to take a specific example of this method of
approach by a well-known social anthropologist. Sir Edmund Leach
wrote an essay, originally delivered as a lecture, entitled 'Why did
Moses have a Sister?' The very title will warn us that we are not to
expect a study in either history or human biology. Instead, in a very
unexpected way, Leach uses as one of his starting-points that long
tradition within Christianity which sees correspondences between
Old and New Testaments: the Church is the Israel of God; Jesus is

the new Moses giving God's law to his followers on the mountain. It is striking, if the historical element is set aside, to note that Moses and Jesus have as their nearest feminine kinswoman to play any part in the story someone with the same name: Miriam/Mary. (At this point there is a typical example of the capacity of this kind of approach to shed an unexpected light. Though Mary is, of course, spoken of as Jesus' mother, it is remarkable how the visual arts illustrate a different kind of perception. In the Michelangelo *Pietà* in St Peter's, Rome, for example, Mary and Jesus are represented as if they were of the same age, with almost identical features— sister and brother rather than mother and son.) Structural similarities can also be detected between the account of the infancy of Moses in Exodus and that of the infancy of Jesus in Matthew, and both are also reminiscent of the myth of the birth of Horus to Isis and Osiris. There is a correspondence between the 'basket' or 'ark' of Moses in the bulrushes and the 'manger' of Jesus' birth (though here it should be noted that reference to a manger occurs only in Luke, and it is not clear whether Leach has overlooked this point or regards it as of no consequence); the Egyptian princess of Exodus 2 is matched by the wise men, particularly if, as in so much Christian tradition, they are thought of as kings; the enemy figure (the Seth of the Horus myth) is in one case Pharaoh, in the other Herod; each unsuccessfully attempts to exterminate all who might thwart his will, but the chosen child escapes—in Jesus' case, to Egypt! The role of Miriam (unnamed in Exod. 2, but assumed to be the sister mentioned by name in Exod. 15: 20) and that of Mary bring out a further correspondence.

Much of this might seem redolent of a rather old-fashioned piety found in books of devotion. Something of the same might perhaps be said about the discussion of the various geographical areas in which the stories of the patriarchs are set, with Egypt as the land of oppression and Palestine as the land of promise, with the wilderness supplying the locale of the 'rite of passage' from one to the other: the deception of Joseph by his brothers and his sale (Gen. 37); the self-revelation of God to Moses in Exodus 3.

Other aspects of the social anthropologist's concerns would not, however, find a place in books of devotion. One of the particular structures of especial importance in the ordering of society is that of kinship, the concern for marriage within the permitted degrees. (We have already noted the importance of this as an expression of holiness.) The ordering of society would be at risk either through marriage to too close a relation (incest) or through marriage with an alien (exogamy). It is thus maintained that a basic theme of the patriarchal myths is the resolution of the dangers brought about by unacceptable unions of each kind. Relations which a later orthodoxy would regard as incestuous play a prominent part in the patriarchal stories; such relations are indeed implicit in any story of human beings descended from a single pair (as the old jibe, 'Who was Cain's wife?', illustrates). Abraham was married to his half-sister (Gen. 20: 12); Lot can only maintain the human race by an incestuous relation with his own daughters (Gen. 19: 30–8); Moses' own parents were aunt and nephew (Exod. 6: 20). All of these unions were of course forbidden by the laws of Leviticus which came to be associated with the name of Moses himself. Other of Israel's ancestors provoked crisis in a different way by 'marrying out' (exogamy); this was true of Joseph with his Egyptian wife (Gen. 41: 45), and of Moses himself (cf. the story of opposition to Moses in Num. 12 because of the Cushite woman whom he had married). As is illustrated by the books of Ezra and Nehemiah, the fact of exogamy was regarded as a very great threat to the legitimate survival of the religious community.

There are other points in the article which could be taken up by way of illustration, but perhaps enough has been said to show that the type of question raised in this use of the biblical material is very different from that found in the historical-critical approach. For some this will be a relief; for others a cause of profound disturbance. There are in any case certain basic issues which are raised by anthropologists which must be taken seriously by those who wish to increase their understanding of the Old Testament.

The issues raised by anthropology

First, both the comparative and the structural approaches to which reference has been made raise the question of the universality of human nature and assumptions. How far are the ethnological survivals described in the fieldwork of Western-trained anthropologists relevant to the society of ancient Israel? How far are the binary oppositions discerned by Lévi-Strauss and his followers so constitutive of human perception as to provide a key to our understanding of biblical texts? Many when reading the Old Testament will find themselves at some points totally nonplussed by the sheer otherness of it all; at other times it will be as if they see themselves, their own reactions and behaviour, reflected as in a mirror. This tension is one which can probably never be totally resolved; anthropology can certainly shed important light upon it.

Secondly, the shift away from primarily historical concerns which we have noted is one which has penetrated into other approaches to the Old Testament. In the next two chapters we shall be concerned with the use made of the Old Testament in liberation theology, in women's studies, and in literary criticism; and these three approaches might be regarded as inherently very different from one another. Yet in each of them an important connecting link is provided by the fact that they share that impatience with primarily historical questions which we have been noting, and prefer rather to look at the structures of the literature as a means of insight.

Thirdly, it may be that the difference noted at the beginning of this chapter between an 'Anthropology of the Old Testament' and 'Anthropology and the Old Testament' is not quite so great as it then appeared. Any proper treatment of the Old Testament's own view of mankind must draw together a mass of apparently conflicting data and draw them into some kind of organized structure in very much the way we have seen anthropologists attempt to do. In the event we may find that the Old Testament provides a view comparable in some ways with the structures of some modern treatments. It is a point which will arise again when we consider the theology of the Old Testament; but first we must look at two very modern approaches to our material.

The Old Testament as Liberation?

So far each chapter of this book has been concerned with the way in which a particular independent discipline—history, archaeology, sociology, and so on—can legitimately be applied to Old Testament study. In this chapter our concerns will be slightly different in various ways.

The fact that two themes rather than one will be considered is of only incidental concern. More important is the point that we shall be looking at two areas of study and reflection which have only become prominent in very recent times. More significant still may be the fact that, whereas the other approaches considered make use of established scholarly disciplines, each with its own particular customs and concerns, here much of the impetus has come from religious and theological reflection.

Theology as liberation

This is most obviously the case with the movement commonly called 'liberation theology'. Its roots are to be found in Latin America. In the centuries following the Spanish (and Portuguese) conquests the Roman Catholic Church came to be strongly established throughout Central and South America, but it was often associated with political regimes which were widely regarded as brutal and corrupt. Though there were many honourable exceptions the Church was generally perceived as more concerned with the maintenance of the status quo than with the proclamation of the gospel, with its frequent challenges to the established order. It was not until the middle years of the present century that that situation came to be subjected to radical criticism.

For a number of reasons the development of this theme of liberation has focused with particular strength on the Old Testament. To some extent an awareness of a parallel between ancient and modern situations of repression can also be traced in negro spirituals, with their use of Exodus and wilderness wandering themes to express the reality of their contemporary situation, and this was taken further as the new ideas developed. This process is often described as 'conscientization', an ugly word for a very important process. It is essentially a determination to make people aware of their own potentiality as human beings, and the reality of the unjust and oppressive situation in which they had been placed. Characteristically such a movement has found expression in group rather than individual concerns, and to this the Old Testament seemed better suited than the New. To be a follower of Jesus has often, rightly or wrongly, been regarded as a matter for individual decision and commitment; the people described in the Old Testament were part of a larger unity, of nation or tribe or extended family. It was that experience which related most closely to the contemporary situation. And so, with a new emphasis on the importance of the Bible as a matter for individual and group study as well as official Church exposition, a new significance came to be given to the Old Testament in a liberation context.

Exodus as deliverance?

The particular focus of that new significance was the Exodus. It is of crucial importance within the Old Testament itself, constantly referred to in the prophets and the Psalms as well as in the book of Exodus. It is the characteristic context in which Yahweh, the God of Israel, is referred to; the Ten Commandments, for example, have as their prologue: 'I am the LORD your God, who brought you out of the land of Egypt, out of the house of bondage' (Exod. 20: 2), and comparable assertions are found in many parts of the Old Testament. The Exodus, that is to say, is pictured as a deliverance from oppression; it is also not too far-fetched to describe it as a process of conscientization, when the Israelites were brought to a recognition of their collective identity and shown the potential of what they might achieve as a people acting in unity. The stories in Genesis describe events which concern individuals, and derive much of their power from that individual context: will Abraham sacrifice Isaac? How will Joseph and his brothers be reconciled? Those in Exodus 1–6, by contrast, illustrate in different ways this bringing together of Israel as a people, under an appointed leader, committed to the worship of the one God and looking forward to a deliverance from the oppression under which they find themselves. Appropriately these stories end with a genealogy (Exod. 6: 14–25) which functions to establish the identity of the people, and this is followed by the stories of the plagues, which tell of the humiliation of the oppressors. This whole account reaches its climax with the deliverance at the 'Red Sea' and the hymn in praise of Yahweh as deliverer:

Sing to the LORD, for he has triumphed gloriously
The horse and his rider he has thrown into the sea. (Exod. 15: 21).

One point of interest here is that this great proclamation of Yahweh's act of deliverance is expressed by a woman, Miriam, and we shall note in the second part of this chapter how this is a pattern which is frequently found in the Bible: the Song of Deborah in Judges 5 commemorates the great defeat of the Canaanite oppressors; just as in the New Testament it is the women disciples of Jesus who first proclaim the defeat of the oppressor, death, through his resurrection (Mark 16: 1–7).

It will at once be apparent that the concerns inherent in this type of approach are very different from the historical issues at stake in much Old Testament study and considered briefly in chapter 3 above. In this context it is of no consequence who the individual Pharaoh may have been who was responsible for the oppression; indeed it may be regarded as positively valuable that the Pharaoh is not identified, for individual sympathies are not engaged, and it is easier to regard him as a representative figure, standing for all unjust and oppressive rulers. It is of no consequence whether the Exodus took place in the fifteenth or the thirteenth century BC; it is the reality of the oppression which is crucial rather than the detailed historical circumstances, the reconstruction of which forms the focus of much modern discussion. It is of no consequence where precisely the deliverance at the sea took place; above, the phrase 'Red Sea' was put in quotation marks, for the deliverance cannot have taken place at the stretch of water nowadays known as the Red Sea, but, for this understanding of the Exodus, discussions as to whether we should think of the Bitter Lakes near the present Suez Canal or some other locale are irrelevant. It is God's mighty act of liberation, deliverance, which provides the model.

This is a use of the Bible which seems strange to many in the West and, when it is grasped, can be profoundly disturbing. We should note straightaway that it is in line with one reading of much of the prophetic material. The prophets, too, showed themselves to be opposed to an established order which they regarded as oppressive. Sometimes this emerges from the stories of the prophets in the books of Samuel and Kings, such as Elijah's confrontation with Ahab after he had taken possession of Naboth's vineyard (1 Kgs. 21: 17–24), sometimes it is clearly implicit in prophetic oracles (Mic. 3 condemns all the ruling groups of his time in the most forthright terms, and is typical of many such texts in the prophets). There is, that is to say, a strongly anti-authoritarian strand in the Old Testament, to which our attention has rightly been drawn afresh by liberation theologians. The book of Amos has come into great prominence in recent years not least because of its overall stance, epitomized in chapter 7, of opposition to the established powers of the day.

Here a tension arises which has often been obscured. The Old Testament is a collection of holy writings, gathered together by the Jerusalem community of the last centuries BC as the embodiment of its sacred traditions. As such it is conventionally bound together in one volume, and our natural expectation is that within the pages of any one book we shall find a consistent viewpoint expressed. That expectation is heightened when the book in question is a 'holy book', regarded by its human authors as expressive of the divine will. But in fact some sharply differing viewpoints are found within the pages of the Old Testament, and nowhere are those differences more acute than when they relate to this theme of liberation.

We have seen that some parts of the Old Testament speak powerfully on behalf of the oppressed: the community as a whole when it is oppressed by foreign tyrants like the Pharaoh of Exodus; groups within the community who are oppressed by the manipulation against them of the legal and social structures which should have maintained their rights, as exemplified particularly in the warnings of the eighth-century prophets. But this is not the whole of the story. We may take as an example differing attitudes to the poor.

Attitudes to the poor

From what has already been said it is natural to find in the prophets frequent reference to the poor as those needing liberation in the sense in which we have been using that term in this chapter. Thus Amos in particular brings together the twin themes of assurance for the poor that they have not been forsaken by their God, and condemnation of the rich as oppressors. Amos 2: 6 is particularly revealing in this connection; the oppressors are condemned

> because they sell the righteous for silver
> and the needy for a pair of shoes.

What is particularly noteworthy here is the way in which 'righteous' and 'needy' are regarded as synonymous; the needy are regarded as acceptable to God. There are many other passages in Amos which condemn those who oppress the poor: the rich women of 4: 1, those engaged in sharp business practice of 8: 4–6. Such concern for the poor is not confined to the prophets; the Torah expresses similar requirements: 'You shall not pervert the justice due to your poor in his suit' (Exod. 23: 6).

But there are other parts of the Old Testament which seem to express a markedly different view. From the book of Proverbs, for example, it would be very difficult to find anything remotely resembling a liberation theology. There the poor are for the most part regarded as feckless:

> A slack hand causes poverty,
> but the hand of the diligent makes rich.   (Prov. 10: 4)

The whole of the book of Proverbs expresses the standpoint of the established in society, for whom property rights are important, for whom prosperity is a clear sign of divine favour. Those who have prospered are indeed urged to show generosity to the poor (Prov. 29: 14; 30: 14), but this is a far cry from the basic challenge to the established order which many have discerned in the prophets. As with Proverbs, much of the argument of the book of Job finds its basis in the fact that the removal from Job of all that he held most dear—family, possessions, health—was an indication of the removal of divine favour. To be reduced to poverty was to be taken away from God's approval. As the book of Job proceeds, of course, this assumption is drastically challenged, though scarcely along the lines of liberation theology; the point remains that here and elsewhere in the Old Testament there is no suggestion that poverty is in itself something desirable. It is an evil to be escaped from, and to that extent liberation may be the appropriate word. But in so far as liberation (and liberation theology) implies the overthrow of the established order, then these parts of the Old Testament would regard such an outcome as disastrous. Proper concern for the welfare of the poor is encouraged, for 'He who is kind to the poor lends to the LORD' (Prov. 19: 17; cf. also 22: 9), but this is an encouragement to charity within a continuation of the established order. It is a commonplace of revolutionary political thought and of liberation theology that such benevolence is deeply suspect, as posing as great a threat to any real change as the most brutally oppressive viewpoints.

It is clear, therefore, that while the Old Testament provides much material with which those struggling for liberation can identify themselves, it is not consistent in such an approach. Something very similar can be found in the different texts relating to kingship. Kingship in the ancient world was not a matter of constitutional monarchy such as is found in some countries today; kingship meant absolute rule. Some parts of the Old Testament recognize this and warn against kingship as an evil (e.g. 1 Sam. 8: 11–18), but elsewhere, notably in the Psalms, the gift of a king is regarded as a clear sign of divine favour. It can be instructive to speculate whether particular passages may be the product of court circles, anxious to plead for the role of the king, whereas others come from strata of society which wished to see a more egalitarian state of affairs; our present concern must be to note that on this extremely important matter the biblical text does not speak with one voice. We must bear in mind that at one level the Old Testament is legitimately regarded as a library or collection of books rather than as an expression of one single viewpoint.

The role of women

This same ambiguity arises in another area which has contributed much to Old Testament study (and indeed biblical study in general) in recent years: that related to the role of women. In 1956 Rose Macaulay, in her delightful novel *The Towers of Trebizond*, wrote of the position of women as 'that sad and well-nigh universal blot on civilisations'; it would be interesting to know whether she foresaw the great upsurge of interest in this whole matter which the next generation would bring. For our present context there are two closely related but distinct matters of concern; first, the way in which women's studies, as an academic discipline in its own right, has affected Old Testament study; secondly, the renewed interest in the place of women in the Old Testament world. The two issues are bound together by the way in which a biblical view has often been taken as a model for a view of society and of relations between the sexes in the contemporary world.

Women's studies and the Old Testament

First, then, we may consider the relation between women's studies and biblical studies. There have been distinguished women biblical scholars in almost all traditional aspects of the discipline, but until recently they have been individuals working in what was essentially a man's world. Since the 1960s that situation has to some extent changed, though it must be said that for the most part the world of biblical studies is still strongly male-dominated. But here as in other academic disciplines a distinctive area of women's studies has emerged, and an important item on its agenda has precisely been to challenge that built-in bias which has represented its subject-matter in exclusively masculine terms. Not simply the practice of referring to God as 'he', but also the characteristically negative implications of many feminine references comes under criticism. Thus the term 'Israel' would naturally be taken as neuter in English (or masculine in Hebrew, which does not have a neuter gender), but the word is often regarded as feminine, particularly when it is used in a condemnatory way. (Here a further problem arises, to which we must return: such condemnations are found in the prophetic books themselves, e.g. Hos. 2; Ezek. 16; and the question must therefore arise whether the anti-feminine bias is not already built into the material being studied.)

In some ways a more basic issue for women's studies arises from the whole attempt to construct a story, a world-view, in which women's role will be understood positively and creatively; and there has been much debate whether in such an attempt the whole Judaeo-Christian tradition is to be regarded as hopelessly misogynist. Some would maintain that the masculine bias is not simply a matter of the interpretative tradition imposed upon the biblical material, but is inherent in that material at every level, and when this view is taken it has even led to attempts to give new life to the worship of those goddesses against whose cult the Old Testament contains such vigorous polemic (e.g. Astarte, or the 'queen of heaven' mentioned in Jer. 44: 19 and elsewhere). Frequently, however, women scholars have regarded this as a misreading of the biblical tradition, and have claimed to be able to discern within it other structures which give a more positive assessment to the role of women. This will arise again when we reach our second consideration; the place of women in the biblical tradition itself. For the moment, however, there are significant contributions from within the field of women's studies to which we should pay attention.

Against the historical-critical method?

The academic study of the Bible in the West for more than 200 years has been dominated by what can broadly be called the historical-critical method. As we have to some extent noted already and shall see more fully in the next chapter that dominance has come under increasing questioning in recent years; and it is surely no coincidence that this shift of emphasis has taken place at the same time as the contribution of women's studies has increased. Traditionally it has been felt that the proper questions to be asked of the biblical text have been: who is its author? (Or more commonly, in practice, is the alleged author also the actual author?) From what date does this text originate? Has it been elaborated or 'tampered with'? What can we know of the historical circumstances underlying the text? Only, it has been maintained, when satisfactory resolutions of such questions as these have been reached can the next step legitimately be taken of the exegesis and application of the text. And in practice that in turn has often meant that the difficulties and differences emerging over the first stage resulted in the next stage never being reached at all.

What has happened to an increasing extent in recent years can best be described as an impatience with this type of detailed study, which places historical questions in a privileged position, and requires critical analysis of a text before other questions can legitimately be addressed to it. Instead, many have determined to look at the text as a whole, as a piece of literary art. Some of the more general issues raised by this kind of approach will occupy us in the next chapter; for the moment we may note that in this type of approach women scholars have played a part out of all proportion to their number, and have brought certain distinctive insights to bear. This can best be illustrated by a specific example.

Hagar

In Genesis 16 and 21 there are two stories relating to Hagar, an Egyptian slave, who bears a child to Abraham when it appears impossible that his wife Sarah will ever have a child. In the first story she is driven away while pregnant by her jealous mistress Sarah; in the second, she is again driven away, this time with her child Ishmael, because by now Sarah has herself borne a son, Isaac, and she and Abraham do not wish any threat to be posed to Isaac's rights of inheritance by his half-brother Ishmael.

Traditional scholarly methods have been applied to these two stories and have raised such questions as: are the two stories really variants of one original? If so, do they help in the source-criticism of Genesis? Are there legal texts either from Israel itself or from neighbouring countries which would shed light, either on the custom of a man begetting a child by a slave-wife, or on the rights of that wife and her child if a legitimate heir were subsequently born?

Can anything be known of the historical background of such stories so as to date the patriarchs with more confidence?

Questions such as these have their own significance. But it has been with the emergence of women's studies, and the application of that kind of 'conscientization' which we saw to be so important in liberation theology, that these stories have been looked at from a different perspective: that of Hagar, the victim. On such a reading, texts of this kind have important messages to convey with reference to the plight of women as victims in a male-dominated and male-structured world. Hagar is summoned without her consent to fulfil her master's pleasure and to bolster his self-esteem, by ensuring that there are offspring through whom his name will be handed down; she is the victim cast out when her presence becomes too great an embarrassment to her master and mistress; she is even the victim of the narrator, for the whole story is told from the point of view of Abraham and Sarah and the tradition they represent, and Hagar plays no further part in the story once her immediate future has been secured. More than one study of this story by a woman scholar has invited us to look at it from an angle different from the traditional one. At one point, however, a curious irony arises: Hagar was an Egyptian; the point is made three times (Gen. 16: 1, 3; 21: 9), and appears to be deliberately stressed. Some modern scholars have taken this point as a cue to identify Hagar, as an African, with the oppressed who seek liberation in the sense already discussed. Yet this would be a very unusual way of reading Old Testament references to Egyptians, who are habitually the oppressors rather than the oppressed. An important truth to be kept in mind is that the Old Testament is liable to resist our attempts to categorize according to our modern presuppositions.

A patriarchal world

It is however clear that the whole Hagar episode does raise once again the question already referred to: the overwhelming patriarchality of the biblical world. As we have just seen, her story is told from the perspective of a narrator for whom the promise of an heir to Abraham (by whatever means, it would almost appear) was the essential point. This is representative of much of the biblical world—though it is also important to remember that in Genesis in particular the role of women is very powerfully portrayed, as in Rebekah's plot to ensure that her favoured son Jacob succeeded Isaac (Gen. 27) and in Rachel's deception of her father in the matter of the 'gods' (Heb. *teraphim*; their nature is much disputed) (Gen. 31), and a variety of smaller episodes. But by and large there is no disputing that the Old Testament world is a strongly patriarchal one.

This point is significant at various levels. At its most basic, it arises from the fact that it is highly probable that all the books which have come down to us have masculine authors. Individual elements are attributed to women, such as the 'songs' of Miriam (Exod. 15: 21), of Deborah (Judg. 5), and of Hannah (1 Sam. 2: 1–10), and this may suggest that women had a specific role in some cultic ceremonies, which involved them, perhaps in the composition, and certainly in the rendering, of such songs of praise. (Ps. 68: 11 is a difficult verse to translate, but the expression rendered 'those who bore the tidings' in RSV is in fact feminine in Hebrew, and is so rendered in some translations; possibly a particular role for women is here alluded to.) But all this is quite a different matter from the final form of the books in which these extracts are now embedded; all that is known of scribal practice and custom suggests that it was a male preserve.

More important is the assumption of male 'normality'; always it is taken for granted that male customs and requirements dictate the patterns of society. Very revealing in this connection, not least because of its great importance in shaping the attitudes of later Western society, is the spelling out of conditions of ritual purity in Leviticus 12–15. These chapters, often neglected because of their unattractive subject-matter, have come to be very significant both for the anthropological approach which we considered in the last chapter, and because of the revealing glimpse they afford as to the basic norms of society in the biblical world. At the very outset we are confronted with male horror on account of female blood; the bearing of a child, the most essential of all facts of life for the future of the community, is regarded as making the mother 'unclean' (Lev. 12: 1), and elaborate rituals have to be completed before that uncleanness is purged. Once again the basic assumptions of the compiler are revealed by the way in which the period of 'uncleanness' lasts twice as long if the baby born is a girl. Then in chapter 15 the same word, *tame*, 'unclean', is used to describe a woman at her time of menstruation; what makes a man 'unclean' is his contraction of a venereal disease! Elsewhere it is striking that when a woman is praised, apparently unreservedly, as in the poem at the end of Proverbs (31: 10–31) it is because of her esteem in male terms. Even in a woman the masculine qualities of shrewdness and far-sightedness may be found, so much so that her husband may indeed be proud of her (vv. 11, 23). It is not surprising that women's studies have drawn attention to these assumptions and shown how one-sided and partial they are.

God as masculine?

But of course the issue of patriarchality goes deeper yet; for it is concerned perhaps most fundamentally of all with the presentation of God in exclusively male terms. Here an issue arises which will occupy us again when we come to consider the development of religious belief and practice in the Old Testament world.

The origins of belief in Yahweh and the nature of his worship remain topics of acute difference of opinion, but it seems clear that he was worshipped in the early period—perhaps down to the time of the great prophets—in essentially masculine terms. Throughout the ancient Near Eastern world gods and goddesses were reverenced who were pictured in a complex series of personal and sexual relations with one another; and Yahweh was emphatically a god in the masculine sense. Possible the 'queen of heaven', to whom we have referred, was envisaged as his spouse; certainly the texts from Kuntillet Ajrud (which will be mentioned again in chapter 9, which deals with religious developments) refer to 'Yahweh and his Asherah' in terms that are most readily understood of a god and his related goddess. At a later stage in the people's history, however, such an understanding was no longer acceptable, and it was the universal characteristics of Yahweh which came to be emphasized. Such a development can clearly be seen in the *shema'*, the prayer still recited daily by devout Jews (Deut. 6: 4), with its emphasis on the oneness of Yahweh. The book of Deuteronomy, and texts edited under Deuteronomistic influence, provide many examples of this claim setting out the universal character of Israel's God, and this may well reflect important theological development at approximately the time of the exile. Even clearer is the evidence from Isaiah 40–55, chapters which were composed among the Babylonian exiles, probably in the 540s; there we find the most profound assertions of the universal character of God. No longer envisaged as a tribal or national God, Yahweh was now the only creator, the only effective God, beyond any claims made on behalf of other deities, incomparable.

The striking fact for our present concerns is that it is precisely in these chapters that the author makes use of feminine images in the building up of the appropriate theological picture. Here God can be described in successive verses first as a man of war and then as one who cries out like a woman in travail (Isa. 42: 13 f.); here too God's love for Zion is directly compared with that of a mother for her sucking child (Isa. 49: 15). Strikingly, therefore, feminine imagery for the deity can be found in the context of the universal claims that were being made on behalf of Israel's God, precisely at the time of her greatest political impotence. Worthy of note here is the role given to wisdom in creation, particularly in Job 28 and Proverbs 8: 22–31. The Proverbs passage is particularly striking, for wisdom herself is pictured as speaking, and emphasizing the vital role she had played in the mighty acts of divine creation. The Hebrew word translated as 'wisdom' is *ḥokmah*, a feminine noun. It is of course very difficult to know how far the gender of a noun is itself significant, but it is certainly clear that wisdom is treated almost as a kind of independent being alongside God in the work of creation; and this too can be seen as one way of asserting a feminine element in the deity. In short, while it would be absurd to suggest that the language used of God is anything other than overwhelmingly masculine, there is enough use of feminine language to warn us that too easy an acceptance of masculine metaphor is likely to be inadequate. (It has proved impossible in this book altogether to avoid reference to God by means of the masculine pronouns 'he', 'him', for no satisfactory alternative has yet been devised; but it needs to be kept in mind that this usage is a limiting one which hides an important part of the biblical perception of God.) Here too women's studies have been of value in broadening perspectives.

The Old Testament perception of women

What of our second question, the place of women in the biblical text itself? To some extent we have touched on this already, for example in the consideration of Hagar, and the understanding of women in the 'uncleanness' texts. But there are more basic issues involved, concerned not just with the accounts of individual women, but with the whole question of the feminine role.

Attention here has characteristically focused upon two texts: the creation stories in Genesis; and the Song of Songs. The Genesis stories in particular provide a fascinating example of some of the difficulties posed when translating from one language to another in which the idioms are different.

Creation stories

It is universally agreed among scholars that the stories in Genesis 1–3 come from two different contexts. The account of creation in Genesis 1: 1–2: 4*a* (to 'when they were created' in RSV), with its highly stylized repetitive format, is commonly regarded as originating from priestly circles and is often labelled 'P', in common with other material in the Torah which betrays similar interests and vocabulary. Genesis 2: 4*b* represents the beginning of a new story, which presents creation in quite different terms, centring around the bringing into being of the first humans, and describing their early history and relation with God. Here, by contrast with Genesis 1, the divine name 'Yahweh' (RSV: LORD) is used throughout, and so this is regarded as a special characteristic of this material. (Somewhat confusingly for English readers this material is usually given the letter 'J' to designate it; this comes from the German rendering of the divine name as Jahveh, and English-speaking scholars have followed the German labelling.)

We have then two sources, each of which has its distinctive way of referring to the creation of human beings. In Genesis 1 humanity is clearly regarded as the crown of creation, for which the whole previous account has been preparing the way. In verse 26 'man' is differentiated from all other created beings by being made in the image and after the likeness of God himself. But it is important to recognize that the word 'man' here stands for the whole of humanity, not simply the male sex. This is made clear in verse 27 where it is specified that 'man' includes both male and female. It is obvious that difficulties arise from the ambiguity of the English word 'man', which has in the past been used to refer to humanity at large as well as to masculine human beings. Whether such a more general usage will continue to be acceptable is a nice question.

But problems of this kind become more acute when we look at the story in Genesis 2–3. Hebrew is unlike English in having two words which normally serve to differentiate between individual masculine human beings and the race as a whole; the word *ish* is used for individuals, the word *adam* for humanity. But clearly this general rule cannot be applied automatically in Genesis 2–3, where *adam* is at some point in the story transmuted into Adam, an individual human being with a partner named Eve. Traditionally this story in Genesis 2–3 has been read from a strongly male-centred viewpoint, with woman totally dependent upon man and inferior to him. Genesis 2: 18–23 is then read so as to stress that woman is comparable with, though superior to, the domestic animals, and the word 'helper' taken to imply lower status. By the same kind of understanding woman is regarded as responsible for the 'fall' of man through her weakness in listening to and being tempted by the serpent (3: 1–13). Readings of this kind have dominated much subsequent exegesis of this story, and thereby have played their part in shaping Christian doctrine. Are such readings fair, or are they themselves vivid illustrations of that male hegemony with which contemporary feminism finds itself at odds? There can be no serious doubt that in the later thought of both Judaism and Christianity this view of woman as inherently inferior to man, and posing a threat to man's capacity for right behaviour, was widespread; one example of such thought in a Jewish context may be found in the Apocryphal book Ecclesiasticus (42: 12–14); from the early Christian tradition the same disparaging attitude is found particularly in 1 Timothy 2: 12–15. But the fact that views of this kind developed does not necessarily mean that they provide the appropriate way of reading the Genesis texts themselves.

There are many levels at which the story of Genesis 2–3 can be read. Thus it has played an important part in the kind of structural anthropological theory to which reference was made in the last chapter. On such a reading great emphasis is placed upon the importance of binary oppositions: most basically that between God and the created world; then that between God and man; that between the created world and the chaos which it replaced; that between human beings and animals; that between the life-giving fruit of the trees in the garden and the death which is said to be the result of eating the fruit of the tree of life. In such a reconstruction the role of the woman could also obviously be construed in a variety of ways: as the mediating figure between man and the animals; as the crown of creation, since the whole thrust of the creation stories is toward a climax; as deliverer of man from the curse of alone-ness; and so on. Such readings can be fascinating but objectivity can scarcely be claimed; the 'myth' may be read in different ways none of which has a claim to be *the* correct one.

We can nevertheless make two suggestions concerning a reading of this text which may help to shed light on some of the problems it raises. First, it is widely recognized that one of the characteristic concerns of Genesis 2–3 is aetiological, that is to say, a wish to explain characteristic features of human life by showing that their origins go back to the very beginnings of human existence. Why do snakes crawl? Why is nakedness commonly associated with feelings of shame? Why is manual work commonly so unrewarding a task?— these and many other issues are explained in Genesis 2–3 in terms which make it clear that these are universal characteristics which go to the roots of existence. One of the most basic of such issues is the difference between the sexes, the different perceptions of the male and female in many of the most basic aspects of life. On such a view it is no coincidence that it was to the woman that the snake spoke, nor is feminine weakness a proper explanation of what took place. Just as it is the female of the species who maintains life through child-bearing, so she is more closely in touch with the earth and its creatures and so it is natural that what we might nowadays call her 'instincts' would be more sensitive to the issues raised by the serpent—which were, after all, real enough issues. An approach along these lines seems to be supported by the character of the divine injunctions in Genesis 3: 14–19, which spell out some of the sexual differentiations implicit in this.

Secondly, the word translated 'helper' (2: 18, 20) is liable to be misunderstood. At first glance it may seem to imply a subordinate role, but it is important to remember that the most common usage of the word relates to God. Frequently in the Psalms God is described as the one who can and will help in trouble:

> I am poor and needy; hasten to me, O God;
> Thou art my help and my deliverer; O LORD, do not tarry.
> (Ps. 70: 5, where the word translated 'help' (*'ezer*) is the same
> as that used in Gen. 2)

Clearly the idea does not of itself imply any kind of subordination; the helper is one who rescues from the perils to which humanity is heir, and that is true of the woman in the garden as well as in the prayers of the psalmist.

The Song of Songs

The only other book of the Old Testament which concerns itself in any direct and positive way with such matters of sexual politics is the Song of Songs. (This literal and almost meaningless translation of the book's Hebrew title should be understood as a superlative; this is the 'best of songs'. The other title found in translations, the Song of Solomon, arises from the fact that the author puts on the conventional identity of Solomon, the son of David (e.g. 1: 1), but there is no serious likelihood that this collection of poems comes from the pen, or even the period, of Solomon.)

It is not possible here to discuss the Song of Songs in detail, but it is worth noting that it takes a very different view of sexuality, and of relations between the sexes, from that which was to become normative in either the Jewish or the Christian tradition. Sexual love is a matter of delight and the charms of the beloved are described with no sense of embarrassment or shame. More relevant for our immediate concern is the way in which the woman can be as direct and as able to take initiatives as the man. Few would suggest that the Song of Songs should be regarded as the most important part of the Old Testament, but it has very great significance in the way in which it challenges received assumptions about the role of the sexes. Perhaps it is not surprising that the Song of Songs has often been appreciated most deeply by those who stand outside the main religious traditions, but have been drawn to it by the beauty of its poetry. It is to that literary power of the Old Testament, which is by no means confined to the Song of Songs, that we must next turn.

8

What Kind of Literature?

Whatever the disagreements about the interpretation of the Old Testament that we have noted in previous chapters, all will agree that the Old Testament is a body of literature. At first sight this might appear to be a relatively uncontroversial statement; in fact, as with practically any literature which has won high esteem this in itself quickly leads to further dispute when interpretation is embarked upon.

Literary criticism: old style

All great literature has given rise to literary criticism; indeed one might be tempted to say that a working definition of great literature would be those writings which have attracted critical attention and scrutiny. In that context the biblical writings would pass the test easily enough. But a curiosity would then emerge. Literary criticism, when applied to the Bible in general and to the Old Testament in particular, has often taken a very unusual form.

This can best be illustrated by referring to the type of book called 'Introduction'. Coming upon a volume entitled 'Introduction to the Old Testament' in a library or bookshop one might expect a general guide to its contents, historical or geographical background, perhaps something about the history of its interpretation. The actual contents of such a book are likely to be quite different. Each book of the Old Testament will indeed receive a section of discussion; but the questions raised about it will be overwhelmingly those related to how the book came to reach its present form, with detailed attention to possible sources, strata, genuine and non-genuine elements, and the like. The Pentateuch in particular has been discussed in this way. 'Pentateuchal Criticism' has not normally meant an assessment and evaluation of the contents of the Torah; instead it has taken the form of detailed analysis of its components, with the usual result that it has been claimed that four distinct sources can be traced, which between them account for almost all of the material that has come down to us. That such an analysis is a necessary preliminary to any further study of the Pentateuch has indeed become almost an article of faith; not to engage in such study has been regarded as a kind of fundamentalist, anti-critical, anti-intellectual stance from which emancipation was necessary. The same kind of approach has also characterized the study of other biblical books; the prophetic collections, in particular, were analysed so as to sift out the (often very small amounts of) 'genuine' material (that is, that which probably could be regarded as the prophet's own words) from the secondary additions in which that material is now embedded.

As we saw in the last chapter, there has been developing something of a reaction against such an approach, which can indeed be very limiting if pursued in isolation. (This book was originally advertised as an 'Introduction to the Old Testament', but its title was changed precisely because of the very limited meaning which this term has come to have.) Without taking the matter further at this point, it is perhaps worth bearing in mind that traditional questions of this kind do still need to be asked, if we are to understand the Pentateuch and the other texts in their historical setting; as we have already discovered, historical questions are not the only kind which should be asked of the Bible but they nevertheless remain important. Those features of the Pentateuch or of the book of Isaiah which make it very difficult to suppose that they could originate from one author remain and need to be addressed, even if we also recognize that other questions can properly be put to these texts, which may enable us to have a different picture of the literary heritage of the Old Testament.

Literary criticism: new style

Such questions have come to assume greater prominence, not least because of the interest taken in the Old Testament by literary scholars with no particular religious commitment. A great deal of such interest has arisen in recent years, for the most part since the mid-1970s, though it is worth bearing in mind that a literary interest in the Bible does go back to a much earlier period. Thomas Hardy, for example, was noting in his Diary in 1884 the 'completeness of perfect art in these Bible lives and adventures' and wondering whether the immediate impression of their truth was necessarily justified: 'Is not the fact of their being so convincing an argument not for their actuality but for the actuality of a consummate artist?' (*The Life and Work of Thomas Hardy*, ed. M. Milgate (Macmillan, 1984), p. 177). This particular point is an important one, for it has often been argued that the experiences of individuals are portrayed so vividly that they *must* therefore be true in the sense that they go directly back to the experience of the individual himself. The court history of David (2 Sam. 9–20, 1 Kgs. 1–2), for example, or the account of Hosea's marital relations (Hos. 1–3), or the psalm-like prayers of Jeremiah sometimes called his 'confessions' (e.g. Jer. 15: 15–18; 20: 7–18) have often been approached in this way. Hardy was himself a marvellous delineator of character, and he knew how possible it was to achieve such results by means of the 'actuality of a consummate artist'.

In recent years, however, this type of interest has increased very markedly, and many studies have appeared of a variety of Old Testament material where the prime concern has been with the literary characteristics displayed. This has usually meant that texts are looked at in their final form, without concern for their previous history or source structure. The insights obtained thereby have been of a kind very different from those of traditional biblical scholarship. Concern with narrative technique, for example, often cuts across any attempt to divide particular sections into disparate sources, or to give confident answers concerning historicity.

A simple example will suffice to illustrate the first point. The last chapters of Genesis (37, 39–50) tell the story of Joseph in Egypt; after his abandonment by his brothers he rises to a position of great honour under the Egyptian Pharaoh; his brothers come to Egypt, at first seeking food in a time of famine. They do not recognize Joseph, but he knows who they are and eventually makes himself known to them. After a number of vicissitudes which heighten the tension, they are reconciled and bring their father, the aged Jacob, into Egypt to settle with them under Joseph's protection. It is a superbly told story, and many literary critics have been concerned to see it as such and to highlight its narrative qualities. Much traditional biblical criticism has, however, claimed to see two or more sources here, woven together into one narrative. Thus in Genesis 48 we are told first that 'Israel [an alternative name for Jacob, and thus possibly an indication of a different source?] saw Joseph's sons' (v. 8), then that 'he could not see' (v. 10), and that this led him to bless the younger son above his older brother. This has been taken by some scholars as a sign of source-division, with differing views on Jacob's ability to see! But many will view such an analysis as hair-splitting, and will be much more interested in the literary comparison made between the blessing by Jacob here and that of Isaac in Genesis 27, again a story of a blind patriarch blessing the expected successor and again a story in which the younger son received the blessing which would normally have gone to his older brother. Each of these stories also brings out another favoured device of Hebrew narrative: the use of word-play. The word for 'first-born' and the verb 'to bless', *bekor* and *berek*, look and sound very similar, and in each of these stories this similarity is prominent. It is of course impossible to bring it out satisfactorily in translation. Other passages in Genesis, both in the Joseph story and in the earlier sections, may profitably be looked at in the same way.

This brings us to the second point mentioned above: the lessening of concern for specifically historical questions. Such an approach raises issues that are predominantly literary rather than historical. A good example can be found in the accounts of Saul and of David in 1 Samuel. Traditionally these stories have been explored so as to achieve a fuller grasp of the circumstances attending the establishment of Israel and Judah as nation-states; the approximate date when this took place; the historical setting, having regard to the apparent non-involvement of any of the surrounding great powers; the various social groups involved in the support of Saul and of David. But clearly it would be possible to approach these stories essentially as *stories*, noting the narrative techniques employed, comparing them with other traditional stories which depict the downfall of one chosen figure and his supplanting by a rival, noting the way in which divine approval/disapproval are used as legitimating devices to uphold the rise to power of the final conqueror. It is clear enough that such an approach raises questions of a very different kind to those engendered by historical criticism; opinions will of course differ sharply as to whether one type of question should be regarded as inherently more important than the other.

God in a story

One aspect of this type of approach is that in a skilfully-told story the features of each of the characters will be outlined. But in these stories it is clear that one of the characters is God. He is presented as one of the participants in the drama, and at times he can be as inconstant and unpredictable as any of the human characters. Thus in 1 Samuel 15 he engages in conversation with Samuel, telling him that he has changed his mind about Saul, whom he no longer regards as an acceptable king. (The RSV translation of 1 Sam. 15: 10f., 'The word of the LORD came to Samuel: "I repent that I have made Saul king"', gives a slightly misleading impression, both in the way that it 'distances' God from Samuel, and in the religious impression given by the word 'repent'. In effect what we are being told in this episode is that God has changed his mind, a point that is repeated for emphasis at the end of the chapter (v. 35).) In the following chapter Saul's black moods are attributed to 'an evil spirit from the LORD' (v. 14); God is once again portrayed in extremely human terms. It is clear that the full significance of episodes such as this cannot be the subject of historical evaluation, and theologically they pose major problems; only a literary approach, without previous historical or theological presuppositions, can readily take this kind of understanding at its face value.

Another important feature of the literary style of the Old Testament is well illustrated by this device, through which God can be introduced as one of the characters in a story. It is sometimes described as the 'omniscience of the narrator'. This is not merely a matter of being able to report private conversations of soliloquies, at which by definition no one but the participants can have been present. It extends further into a knowledge of God's demands and requirements; as we have seen, in many Old Testament narratives God plays a prominent part as if he were another human actor. Thus, for example, the story of the testing of Abraham (Gen. 22) begins: 'God tested Abraham and said to him'. The narrator, that is to say, knows both God's motivation (that what he was commanding was a test of Abraham) and the details of his conversation with Abraham; and similar examples can be found throughout the Abraham and Jacob stories of Genesis 12–36, though, interestingly enough, to a much smaller extent in the stories of Joseph in Egypt which immediately follow. There a different narrative technique is used.

Interrelated stories

Another aspect of the narrative art of the Old Testament is perhaps less controversial. Though it will be natural to look at each biblical book as the appropriate literary unit, there will often be occasions when our appreciation of an episode in one book depends on the recognition of similarities with another episode elsewhere. Thus the story of the central figure in a narrative finding a wife among the young women who come to draw water at the communal well is found three times (Gen. 24 for Isaac and Rebekah; Gen. 29 for Jacob and Rachel; Exod. 2 for Moses and Zipporah). Each of these stories needs to be read for all the nuances and allusions to be detected. Again the golden calf story in Exodus 32 has an elaborate series of interrelationships with the story of Jeroboam's golden calves when the kingdom was divided (1 Kgs. 12), and that story in turn shows similarities with threatened divisions during David's rule (2 Sam. 20). In all of these cases (and other examples could be cited, e.g. Gen. 19 and Judg. 19, two horrifying stories of the abuse of hospitality rights; 2 Kgs. 12 and 22, two accounts of repairs to the temple) we may feel that historical questions become almost unanswerable; the stories reflect a particular literary technique which should be recognized in those terms.

The intentions of the author

At this point we need to bear in mind another controversial issue, though here the controversy has its roots in literary criticism itself. It is relevant to all forms of serious literature, but especially so for the Bible, regarded by so many as an authoritative text. It concerns the intention of the author. Traditional biblical scholarship has often been regarded in Church circles as threatening, being seen as liable to break down the certainties of established belief, but at least there has been agreement about the importance of grasping the intention of the original author. There might be disagreement as to which parts of a prophetic book go back to the prophet himself; there would be general acceptance that when the original words of the prophet were agreed upon, then the establishing of the intention of the prophet in speaking or writing them was a legitimate and important part of the scholarly task.

With this approach, however, many literary critics have expressed dissatisfaction. For them, any piece of literature must be allowed to 'speak for itself', and questions of the author's intention are irrelevant. What matters is what we discern as we read. If this viewpoint is accepted (and it has long been a matter of sharp debate in literary-critical circles) then clearly any objective criteria for assessing, say, the authority of the Bible, or some part of it, are almost impossible to attain; what remains is simply our own interpretation.

Important also is the way in which such a rejection of the possibility of reclaiming the intention of the original writer would cut across a great deal of traditional biblical study. We may, for example, read the account of the Exodus and admire its quality as narrative: the way in which in Exodus 7–11 the conflict between Moses and the Pharaoh becomes more acute as the plagues take their toll, with the increasing recognition among many of the Pharaoh's own subjects of the power of the forces behind Moses; the drama of the Israelites' escape from Egypt following the confusion brought about by the death of the first-born; the vivid picture of the crossing of the sea itself and the death of the pursuing Egyptians. As story this has a powerful claim on our attention. But it would surely be very strange to suppose that the author's intention was of no significance here, for this story arose out of a profound belief in the capacity of Israel's God to save his people from their distress; all this becomes irrelevant if the pursuit of the original intention is a chimera. We do not have to share the beliefs of the original author(s), and indeed they contain certain aspects and expressions which we should not expect to share; it remains true that without some sense of the deep religious conviction which underlay the composition of this and many other biblical texts our appreciation of them even at the purely literary level will be unnecessarily limited. This whole area of objectivity and intentionality is full of pitfalls for the unwary; discussions in this field are currently one of the most lively and at times delicate aspects of biblical study.

The limits of history

There is one aspect of this literary approach to which we should give some further attention; it relates to the tension between the demands of historical verification and those of literary structure. Again it is to some extent a matter of a challenge to established methods of study, but this issue is by no means a new area of controversy; it arose as long ago as the time at which, for example, the historical accuracy of the accounts of creation or the story of Jonah first came to be doubted. That is to say, it has long been recognized that there are certain parts of the Old Testament which cannot realistically be approached purely in historical terms; and when that point is reached attention very naturally turns to the literary form of the particular section, to see if its message can be conveyed to us by some other means.

A parallel might be drawn here with some of the characters portrayed in, for example, the plays of Shakespeare. It may well be possible to establish that Macbeth was in one sense a 'genuine historical character', but few would regard the prime point of studying or watching that play as a concern with Scottish history; the play's the thing! Even if one turns to the 'historical plays' it is clear that the character of, say, Henry V takes its reality from the literary presentation; it would be a real loss if at each scene one were to engage in minute comparisons with historical 'reality'. The play engenders its own reality.

Is it legitimate to approach biblical characters in the same way? Can one, for example, see the developing presentation of Moses in the Torah in these terms, recognizing the apparent attribution of authorship to Moses himself in these books as a skilful piece of literary craftsmanship? Some will welcome such an approach as a release from what can often seem rather sterile historical questioning; others will regard such comparisons between the Bible and secular literature as a dangerous derogation of its authority. For them, the historical has a dimension of reality which cannot under any circumstances be replaced. (In passing, it is worth recalling again that much literary criticism of the type just described is undertaken by those with no Church or religious commitment, whereas traditional biblical scholarship has for the most part been more closely linked with the Church; this obviously increases the suspicion with which many of these developments are viewed in a Church context.)

Belief through story

There are, however, aspects of literary criticism which may appear to be less controversial in their impact, though, as will become apparent, they too raise very delicate issues. One such arises in terms of the nature of the beliefs expressed by the Old Testament about God and the world. In most parts of the Christian tradition such beliefs are expressed in the form of creeds: statements of faith which characteristically begin 'I [or 'We'] believe in God' and go on to assert a series of propositions about God and about humanity. The Old Testament has nothing of this kind; the proposal has been made that the 'response' in Deuteronomy 26: 5–9 could be understood as a kind of creed, a profession of faith from early Israel, but (even if it be accepted as a formulation separable from its context, which has been questioned) it is clearly very different in form from any Christian creed. Nor can the *shema'*, the prayer recited daily by observant Jews (Deut. 6: 4), be regarded as credal in form.

The characteristic manner of expressing belief about God in the Old Testament is by means of stories. Thus instead of the proposition 'maker of heaven and earth' found in the Christian creed we have the stories in Genesis 1 and 2 of God's creative activity. The assertion which speaks of Yahweh as Israel's God 'from the land of Egypt' at the beginning of the Ten Commandments (Exod. 20: 2) and in the prophetic literature (Hos. 12: 9 and elsewhere) is a way of recalling a story—the story of the Exodus. The God of the Old Testament is a God of promise; and this is described by means of the stories in Genesis which speak of promise to the patriarchs of a son and many descendants, and of a land which will be their inheritance. The nature of the relationship between God and humanity is explored by means of a story—the book of Job. And so one could go on. At first sight it might appear as if the prophetic books form an important exception to this general pattern, but it is striking how they also use story forms to describe aspects of the prophetic message: Amos 7 to show the misplaced confidence of those who suppose that God is always on the side of organized religious practice; Hosea 1–3 as a way of exploring the relation between God and people through a story of marital infidelity. Isaiah, Jeremiah, and Ezekiel all provide further examples of the crucial importance of story in conveying the picture of the kind of God whom the people served and the nature of his dealings with that people.

Such a use of story is undoubtedly attractive, but not without its problems. If the stories are to be given the significance we have suggested, the question immediately arises: must they be historically true for their message to be valid? On this question there will be no consensus: many will feel that the attempt to validate stories of the kind described by claiming their historical reliability is a misdirected effort: the stories have their own message, regardless of whether we should classify them as fact or fiction. For others, the reliability of every historical detail is crucial for their faith. And of course there are many intermediate positions: many who would not feel that the story of Jonah in the belly of the fish has to be accepted literally would still regard it as at least disturbing if it could in any way be shown that the whole Exodus story was a product of literary imagination, with no historical basis.

But to use terms such as these might be taken to imply that the story-teller's art was a purely objective matter. It is of course not so. In any well-told story our sympathies are engaged, our imagination stimulated, we are invited to reflect upon our own situation in the light of the story (or may indeed find ourselves doing so willy-nilly). The wonderful economy with which the story of Abraham's willingness to sacrifice his only son Isaac is narrated (Gen. 22) is in many ways more powerful than would have been a detailed description of the feelings of all the characters. But what is the relation of this to religious faith? Judgements of this kind are inevitably subjective; there are no objective criteria to be called upon. If someone were to say, on hearing the story of Abraham, that he was mad and should have been forbidden to have any future access to his child for fear that he would treat him in such a way again (and that would certainly be the case under the legislation of most modern Western societies), there would be no objective grounds on which the claims of the story could be upheld. Some will be repelled by the story, others will see in it a more profound insight into human character.

The implications are obvious: some will maintain that so subjective a basis cannot be satisfactory when religious faith is at stake, others will recognize in this invitation to a judgement an analogy with the way in which they arrive at religious faith, as a matter of insight into the world in which they live rather than as assent to a series of objective propositions. A story can put both sides of a question in a manner that is not possible in a creed. It is easy to see why many committed believers regard a literary approach of the kind outlined as dangerous.

Prose and poetry

This difference of view is likely to remain, but we can perhaps gain some light on the issues involved if we approach them from what may seem a slightly unexpected direction: the relation of poetry to prose in the biblical tradition. Probably all of us come to poetry with different literary expectations from those with which we approach prose. In many older translations of the Bible no distinction is made between prose and poetry; the whole is set out in chapters and verses in an undifferentiated manner. But in fact the Old Testament contains a rich variety of literary forms within it, and our awareness of this will at once help in our appropriate response to the text.

We noted above (ch. 2) that one of the distinctive characteristics of Hebrew poetry is parallelism: the repetition of synonymous or contrasting ideas in successive lines of a poem as a means of heightening literary effect. It is clearly important to recognize this as a literary device rather than as a basis for factual assertion. Thus, when we read that

> A wise son makes a glad father,
>> but a foolish son is a sorrow to his mother   (Prov. 10: 1)

we recognize that the two lines are making the same point by means of an antithesis; it would be absurd to deduce that a foolish son is acceptable to his father, or that a mother has no pleasure in a wise son. Not all examples are so obvious, but it remains important to recognize the allusive, indirect quality of poetry.

At times it appears as if this quality was obscured even before the biblical tradition reached its final form. Thus, in Joshua 10 there is an account of a battle between Joshua and the Amorites, which reaches a climax with the fervent prayer of Joshua, expressed in poetic form, that the sun would postpone its usual time of setting in order that the Israelites might complete the slaughter before their remaining enemies escaped under cover of darkness (v. 12). In the final form of the text this piece of poetry has been transposed into a statement of fact, that 'the sun stayed in the midst of heaven, and did not hasten to go down for about a whole day' (Josh. 10: 13).

It is arguable that something similar has happened with the accounts of an event of even greater importance for Israel: the crossing of the Red Sea. It would be widely agreed that the poetic version in Exodus 15 is the oldest account that we have, and there we find the description of the disaster that befell the Egyptians:

> Pharaoh's chariots and his host he [Yahweh] cast into the sea,
>> and his picked officers are sunk in the Red Sea.   (Exod. 15: 4)

(The use of poetic parallelism is very clear in this verse.) On this occasion the prose account precedes the poetic version, but is again

quite likely to be an elaboration based on the older poetry, reaching
its climax with the statement that 'the waters covered the chariots
and the horsemen and all the host of Pharaoh . . . not so much as
one of them remained' (Exod. 14: 28). Here as elsewhere it is
important for our understanding of the material to recognize the
literary form with which we are confronted, and not to treat poetry
in the same way as we should a sober prose account. If we bear in
mind that a great deal of the Old Testament is poetry, the
expectations that we bring to our reading of it will be significantly
changed.

Problems of translation

There is a good deal else which could be said of this whole literary
approach to the Old Testament, which has been so long neglected
by those professionally concerned with biblical studies. Only one
other point can, however, be mentioned here: the vexed question of
differing translations of the Old Testament. It is striking that the
most substantial recent literary guide to the Old Testament bases
itself upon the Authorized Version of 1611 rather than on any more
modern translation; literary quality has there been rated as more
important than immediate intelligibility or even accuracy. It can at
once be seen how controversial a decision this is. No doubt the AV
has been of enormous importance in the development of the
language, and allusions to it are all-pervasive in the poetry and
much of the prose of the seventeenth and later centuries. It can
reasonably be said that one's education in English literature is
incomplete without an adequate knowledge of the AV. Yet
questions will soon obtrude; is *that* the reason for reading the Bible?
To improve one's acquaintance with English literature? To
become more aware of the niceties of literary style? There is
certainly a case for regarding such heightened aesthetic awareness
as an important part of religious sensitivity, but it is also true that
more directly religious reasons for reading the Old Testament will
be put forward. The Bible may not now be regarded as once it was,
as a direct guide to moral conduct; nevertheless, its position as the
basis for much religious practice continues to provide a fundamental

reason for contemporary interest in it, and it is to the presentation of the religion of ancient Israel and the theological implications that can be drawn from that presentation that we must turn in our remaining chapters.

9

What Kind of Religion?

We saw in the last chapter that many of those who have contributed to the literary study of the Old Testament have not themselves been moved by any particular religious commitment, and the same is no doubt true of many of those who find such an approach the most rewarding. Yet it remains the case that probably a majority of those who wish to engage at a serious level with the Old Testament will come to it in some religious context, and it is undeniable that the concerns of the Old Testament itself are overwhelmingly religious. Even in those parts of the collection which have sometimes been described as 'humanistic', such as the wisdom books, especially Proverbs, the links with religious concerns are never far away.

In our last two chapters we will therefore address some of these religious concerns, and this may most conveniently be done in two ways. First, in the present chapter, we will look at some developments in the study of the religion of ancient Israel itself (for here, as we have noted in other areas of study, much has been changed as a consequence of modern discoveries of different kinds); then in the next chapter we will consider some of the ways in which attempts have been made to construct modern theological understandings which incorporate insights from that ancient religious system. The two concerns inevitably ov- ᵖp to some extent, since what is perceived to be of importance in the eligion of ancient Israel will often be granted such a status on the basis of a particular modern theological viewpoint; but in principle at least the two approaches seem sufficiently distinct to warrant separate treatment.

The distinctiveness of Israel's religion

Our understanding of the religion of ancient Israel must in effect be shaped by two perceptions which would seem at first glance to be sharply at odds with one another. On the one hand Israel and Judah were two of the small nation-states which occupied a particular part of the territory which we can call Syria-Palestine, whose political vicissitudes very much reflected the pressures imposed by the great powers and whose institutions were not perceived by any contemporary witnesses as being different in kind from those of their neighbours. This is quite unlike the picture that we obtain from, for example, the apocryphal book Judith, which probably dates from the first century BC. There the Ammonite captive Achior warns the Assyrian general Holofernes that it is impossible for him to defeat the Jews if they are being loyal to their religion, 'for their Lord will defend them, and their God will protect them' (Judith 5: 21). Such a statement has no parallel in texts which come from the time of the wars themselves; Judith presents a view of the people's history from a very much later perspective.

On the other hand the fact remains that there appears to have been some feature in Israel's religion which enabled it to survive when the religious systems of all its neighbours disappeared. Moab, for example, probably lost its independence as a result of Babylonian invasion at approximately the same time as did Judah, but we know of no protracted survival of Moabite religious institutions and practice on the grounds that this disaster had been brought about by Moab's god in order thereby to show his control of history. Yet this was the kind of claim which very soon came to be made on behalf of Israel's God in a situation of apparently total defeat and despair. In Jeremiah 27: 6, for example, we find the words put into the mouth of Yahweh: 'I have given all these lands into the hand of Nebuchadnezzar, my servant'. It is clear that this is a theological claim; there is no suggestion that Nebuchadnezzar ever became a 'servant' of Yahweh in the sense of being one of his worshippers.

We are, that is to say, confronted with evidence of two sharply conflicting types. There is much which enables us to construct a kind of religious 'map' of the ancient Near East and to place Israel upon that map, and the similarities which permit this and the fruitful comparisons to which it leads have deepened our understanding of many features that were previously obscure in the Old Testament itself. On the other hand we have to decide how to evaluate those parts of the Old Testament which emphasize the difference between Israel and all its neighbours. We are confronted with that same problem of claims to uniqueness which we considered in chapter 5.

To some extent this tension with regard to religious practice may be eased by the recognition that what has come down to us in the Old Testament represents a kind of 'official version' of the people's religion rather than an objective, dispassionate account of what actually took place at the different sanctuaries and holy places. There will have been a polemical element underlying our documents, a concern to show that a particular interpretation of God's commands was the only proper one, and in that sense it is legitimate to trace a distinction between 'the religion of ancient Israel' in the sense of what actually took place in terms of religious practice, and 'the religion of the Old Testament', the official view of what was done or should have been done.

In ways like this some easing of the tension we have described is perhaps possible; it is doubtful whether it can ever finally be resolved. For the present purpose our most useful approach may be, while keeping that tension in mind, to look first at those aspects of Israel's religion which place it securely in its immediate historical and cultural context, recognizing at the outset that these are the points which may well be played down in the 'official' texts that have come down to us; then to consider the implications of some of those passages which stress the difference between Israel and its neighbours.

The priesthood

Perhaps the most convenient division will be to consider first religious personnel, then religious practice, and then religious belief. Clearly all that can be set out here will be an indication of some of the main points, particularly those which have given rise to dispute. That emphasis is not the result of a deliberate seeking for difficulties, but a reminder of the fact that the written records of ancient Israel, like those of almost any society, will be fullest precisely in those areas where disputes arise; where all are in agreement as to a matter of everyday practice, there will be no incentive to set a particular viewpoint down in written form.

This can be well illustrated by reference to priesthood. In Israel as in all the surrounding states there were specific duties which were to be carried out by priests. The priesthood in Israel never established itself as a sacred caste, set over against the laity, as it did in some states, but its role was nevertheless an important one, as can be seen from the claims made for it in the book of Leviticus. By the end of the Old Testament period the high priest in Jerusalem was in effect the head of the community.

But who might be a priest? It is a recognized characteristic of religious polemic to question the legitimacy of the ministry of those to whom one is opposed, and the Old Testament provides ample evidence of this. Thus, part of the Jerusalemite polemic against what was regarded as dangerous religious innovation at the time of the division of the kingdom was the fact that Jeroboam, the northern king, 'appointed priests from among all the people, who were not of the Levites' (1 Kgs. 12: 31). The assumption here is that to establish one's right to priesthood meant establishing one's status as a Levite, and that seems to be borne out by expressions such as that found in Deuteronomy 18: 1: 'the Levitical priests, that is, all the tribe of Levi'. In fact, not all Levites were able to establish priestly claims, and we hear in Ezekiel 44: 10 of 'Levites who went . . . astray from me', and in the following verses they were to be confined to the more menial tasks of the sanctuary.

In the end it was those who could set out a genealogy going back to Aaron who were able to establish their priestly rights, but even this did not preclude bitter divisions. The strange story in Leviticus 10: 1–3, where two of the sons of Aaron, Nadab and Abihu, are said to have been 'devoured' for wrong cultic practice, must surely reflect further antagonisms between different groups each claiming priestly status. Priesthood, that is to say, conferred certain important privileges which made it an end eminently worth seeking, and this will have provoked rivalries of the kind outlined.

It may incidentally be worth remarking that these concerns for legitimate priesthood throw some light on one of the most prominent—and, to some, alien—features of the Old Testament: the genealogies. These long family lists are important, not only as establishing identity and continuity, but also as making clear the membership of what is regarded as the true community, and with regard to priesthood they had an enhanced significance. For priesthood was something handed down within a family, not a matter of the selection of duly chosen candidates for ordination, and thus to be able to establish one's claims by means of the appropriate genealogy was essential. (Ezra 2: 59–63 provides a vignette of the problems that arose when the proper genealogies could not be traced.) We need also to bear in mind that genealogy could be a creative art rather than an exact science, and there is evidence from the ancient Near East of the use of professional genealogists to establish one's right to a particular status. In the Old Testament there are many examples of the way in which genealogies developed, and we can see one instance of this in the case of Samuel. In the description of his family in 1 Samuel 1: 1 there is no suggestion of any priestly rank, but part of the point of the stories that follow is to make it clear that he was called to an acceptable priesthood; then in the later genealogies he is given priestly descent and linked with the Jerusalem temple staff (1 Chr. 6: 28–33). The genealogies may never be the most immediately attractive parts of the material; they nevertheless provide fascinating insights into the development of the community's traditions.

To return to the role of the priesthood. We are here in one of the areas where Israel's religious practice can be placed most securely within the larger context of the ancient Near Eastern world. Throughout that world priests played a vital role as intermediaries between the divine and the human. If divine guidance was sought in matters of individual or community concern then it was the priests to whom recourse was had.

Two examples from the Old Testament, out of many possibilities, may illustrate this priestly role. In early Israel the priests had charge of the 'urim and thummim'; their exact nature is unclear, but they must have been oracular devices, giving 'yes' or 'no' answers to specific requests for guidance (1 Sam. 14: 41). (It may be that there was also a third possibility: 'no answer', as seems to be implied by 1 Sam. 28: 6, where Saul had received no answer to his requests for guidance.) It is easy to see how such control of the means of access to the divine will might give the priesthood control of many aspects of life, and it is striking that when Israel was established as a state we hear relatively little of this means of conveying the divine will which might have been regarded as a threat to royal institutional religion. Indeed, Ezra 2: 63, to which we have already referred in the context of true genealogies, seems to imply that access to 'urim and thummim' was no longer available.

Another priestly role in bringing messages from God to the worshipper can only be worked out by inference, but its existence seems to be beyond serious dispute. Many Psalms begin with the worshipper pouring out a lament before God, using vivid metaphors of sickness, oppression, betrayal, and the like; Psalms 22, 69, and 88 are just three of many examples. Many such Psalms show a complete change of mood during their course, so that they end on a note of triumphant confidence. It seems highly likely that this change has been brought about by some word or action on the part of the priest as a reassurance to the worshipper that his prayers have been heard and his ills (of whatever kind they may have been; and the metaphors rarely allow us to be sure about this) removed. Occasionally a priestly oracle of this kind is incorporated in the Psalm as it has come down to us (e.g. Ps. 55: 22); more frequently the change is not marked by any formal indication in the text (e.g. the change in Ps. 22 following v. 21).

This role of the priest can be carried a stage further in terms of what was to become the priestly ministry *par excellence*: that relating to sacrifice. As we have seen in an earlier chapter some light can be shed on the basic motivations in the offering of sacrifice by anthropological study, but by the later Old Testament period the requirements for the offering of sacrifice had come to be very precisely codified and many of them are laid down in the early chapters of Leviticus. There it is claimed that no sacrifice could be properly offered unless the priest played his appointed role; whether such claims were universally accepted we have no means of knowing, but it is clear once again that in Israel as in other ancient societies the priesthood was determined to assert its key position as intermediary between God and his human worshippers. After the first Jerusalem temple was destroyed in 587/6 BC blueprints were drawn up which could be put into effect when the temple could be restored (Ezek. 40–8); perhaps something similar took place after the destruction of the second temple in AD 70, but if so opportunity to rebuild never did arise and the blueprints have left no certain trace, though parts of the great Jewish interpretative code, the Mishnah, have been interpreted in this way.

The role of the king

For a modern reader it may seem surprising to find kingship listed among Israel's religious institutions, but here again we find much in common between Israel and its neighbours in the ancient Near Eastern world. Like the priest, the king claimed to be the vital intermediary, the channel of grace, between the god and the community. In the Old Testament we find differing views of kingship, and this is no doubt at least partly due to the fact that in human terms kingship proved to be a failure: the nation lost its independence and was forced to serve foreign rulers, and it was natural enough that the king should receive the blame for this. (Whether a modern assessment would agree with the verdicts handed down on individual kings in the biblical books of Kings is another matter; often it seems as if those whose political skills enabled them to keep their kingdom intact are condemned (e.g. Manasseh, 2 Kgs. 21), and those whose opportunism in the interests of an aggressive religious policy led to disaster are nevertheless praised (e.g. Josiah, 2 Kgs. 23: 29 f.)

The books of Kings make it clear that the king really was the effective head of state and no mere figurehead, and that this control extended to the area of religious practice: the building of the temple was an initiative taken by Solomon, the reform of its worship was instigated by kings, whether in a manner condemned by the author of the books of Kings (e.g. Ahaz, 2 Kgs. 16) or approved by him (e.g. Josiah, 2 Kgs. 22–3). But it is to the Psalms that we must turn if we are to have any real understanding of the role claimed for the king in the religious life of the community.

One Psalm appears to accord divine status to the king: the Hebrew text of Psalm 45: 6 has 'your throne, O God, is for ever and ever' in a context where the king is clearly being addressed. Perhaps this reading should be accepted as part of the adulation of the monarch by his courtiers, but most modern translations modify the sense in some way, such as RSV 'your divine throne endures for ever and ever'. If this passage is disputed there are many others where the sense is clear. Psalm 2: 7 describes the king as God's son, in a kind of adoption formula; Psalm 110: 4 claims priestly rights on behalf of the king; Psalm 89: 3 f., 19–37 pictures the king as the one with whom God makes his covenant, to be mediated through divine favour to the people at large; Psalm 72 combines the theme of the king as universal conqueror with an idealized picture of the blessings brought about to his own people through his beneficent rule.

It is extremely difficult to know whether claims of this kind were generally accepted. As we have seen there is no doubt that the king was head of state in more than a merely formal sense, and in the ancient world religion and politics were bound together much more closely than would usually be the case in the modern West. Even so, it would seem as if some of these claims should best be understood as the exaggerations of courtly language. When in our next section we turn to the role of prophets we shall see that one of their functions could be understood as being a check on those pretensions of kings which came to be regarded as excessive. Amos 7: 10 f., Hosea 8: 4, Micah 3: 9 f., and much in the book of Jeremiah give us a picture of prophets as being opposed to royal claims. Only Isaiah offers a partial exception; he too can be fiercely condemnatory of the reigning king (Isa. 7: 3–9), but he appears to share something of the ideology underlying the royal Psalms in his expressions of hope for an ideal king (Isa. 9: 2–7; 32: 1–5). (Both of these psalm-like passages may in fact come from a period later than Isaiah himself, but the whole Isaiah tradition in which they stand is associated with Jerusalem and its temple, and hence with the Psalms, to a greater extent than any other prophetic collection.)

In its understanding of kingship, therefore, it would be difficult to claim that Israel was significantly different from its neighbours. It would be unwise to suppose that the so-called period of the judges, before there was any king in Israel, represented some kind of alternative constitutional experiment. The different 'judges' were basically military heroes winning battles at a time before the people had come together as a coherent whole, and their achievement, in so far as it can be assessed historically, seems largely to have been in terms of bringing the scattered elements of the people together into a position where central government became a possibility.

The prophets

If a claim to distinctiveness were being made among Israel's religious personnel, it is almost certainly to the prophets that most would look. (We have already given attention to some of the problems arising from the role of prophets (ch. 5), so only brief discussion is possible here.) In Judaism 'the Prophets' is, as we have already noted, the name given to a substantial part of the canon of the Hebrew Bible; in traditional Christianity the Old Testament has regularly been seen as prophetic, pointing forward to a fulfilment in Jesus of Nazareth, or in the Church, or at the end of the age. In one tradition of modern critical scholarship 'prophetic religion'—ethical monotheism, stressing the Fatherhood of God and the Brotherhood of Man—has been seen as the heart of the Old Testament; more recently the prophets have been viewed as the great exemplars of the claims to liberation from oppression. And many other different understandings of the prophetic role could be put forward.

Volume 4 in this series (J. F. A. Sawyer, *Prophecy and the Prophets of the Old Testament* (OUP, 1987)) explores the prophetic tradition more fully than is appropriate here; at this point we may simply note that, despite the great authority which the words of the prophets came to have, their actual status in Israelite society and their relation to religious practice remain far from clear. They are certainly envisaged as divine messengers, proclaiming words from God to individuals and to the whole community. The so-called 'messenger formula', 'thus saith the LORD', is the most frequently found introduction to their words. But it is much more difficult to be certain whether they had an identifiable role in society, and, if so, how that role related to the religious practice of the different sanctuaries.

This can be illustrated by the variety of backgrounds from which different prophets apparently emerged: Amos is called a shepherd (Amos 1: 1) and a herdsman (7: 14); Jeremiah and Ezekiel are both described as priests (Jer. 1: 1; Ezek. 1: 3). Sometimes a prophet seems to have been associated with a particular place, as with Ahijah of Shiloh (1 Kgs. 11, 14), or Isaiah, whose ministry seems to have been confined to Jerusalem; sometimes he might be found in a variety of places (e.g. Elijah; cf. esp. 1 Kgs. 18: 7–15). Indeed, it is by no means self-evident that all those described as prophets in the Old Testament were of the same type. In the books of Samuel and Kings it is noteworthy that we have stories relating the activities of prophets whose links are for the most part with court and cult; then we have a series of 'books' named after individual prophets, containing relatively little biographical detail (and what little is found is almost always provided as illustration of some aspect of the message), but offering instead a collection of oracular material in which it seems as if additions have been made to whatever nucleus goes back to the prophet himself. Some modern scholars have seen a fundamental difference between the two types of prophet; this seems unlikely, but at least we may recall the tendency, already noticed, to give many of the faithful servants of God the title of 'prophet'. This may suggest a conscious identifying of prophecy as *the* way in which God spoke to his people, and would suggest caution in attempts to identify too precisely the historical role of prophets in Israel's religion.

This can be well illustrated by one point: the ambiguity of the attitude of the prophets toward cultic worship. Harsh condemnations can be found, both in the narratives in Samuel and in the prophetic books, of contemporary cultic practice. 1 Samuel 15: 22 and Isaiah 1: 11–15 are typical examples of this condemnation, yet elsewhere both Samuel and Isaiah are found as involved in the cultic practice of their time. (In the case of Isaiah, this admittedly makes certain assumptions about his linkage with the Jerusalem temple as the place of his vision in ch. 6, but it is difficult to see what other reading of the passage is plausible.)

It would certainly be ill-advised therefore to envisage Old Testament prophets as if they were liberal Protestants born out of due time who rejected all forms of sacrificial worship. Though, as we have seen, their status is unclear and may not be precisely definable, nevertheless it seems highly probable that many of them had a relation with the cultic worship offered at the different local sanctuaries. Their role may at times have been a critical one, warning the ministers of the sanctuary against too easy an assumption that they had automatic access to God's favour, but it would be wrong to divorce them altogether from cultic practice. It may be that it is in this capacity for self-criticism that an important aspect of Israel's religious uniqueness can be detected. For the moment, however, we are concerned with description rather than evaluation, and it is to the consideration of religious practice that we are led by this apparently ambiguous position held by the prophets. What do we understand by these words 'cult'/'cultic' which we have been using?

Religious festivals

In the modern world, and particularly in those parts which have come under the influence of the great 'religions of the book', Judaism, Christianity, and Islam, religious practice may often be a matter of carrying out the precepts of the 'holy book'. But that would not be true of ancient Israel, even though it was there that the idea of a 'holy book' apparently first took root. (Note the great veneration given to the 'book of the law' in 2 Kgs. 22–3; it is taken for granted that the demands of the book are those of God and are to be obeyed.) Basically, however, in Israel as in surrounding states, religion in the Old Testament period meant the proper performance of appropriate rites; religion meant cult.

Here we at once find a good example of the tension which we have already noted, between actual practice and the idealizing picture offered by the text in its present form. It is clear that three major festivals were observed: Passover and Unleavened Bread; Weeks; and Tabernacles. The Pentateuch contains several cultic calendars (Exod. 23: 14 ff.; Lev. 23; Deut. 16) which emphasize the importance of the proper observance of these festivals. It would be easy at first glance to suppose that these observances characterize Israel's uniqueness, for each of them is linked in some way with the great historical events of the people's past: Passover with the deliverance from Egypt; Weeks with the encounter with God at Mount Sinai; Tabernacles with the time of wandering in the wilderness.

Upon reflection, however, it soon becomes clear that it is not so easy to take these festivals as pointers to Israel's unique position. For a start they are all agricultural festivals, with Passover commemorating the beginning of barley harvest, when the old leaven was cleared away, Weeks marking the beginning of wheat harvest some seven weeks later, and Tabernacles the joyful autumn festival when all the harvest had been gathered in, including that of the vine. Festivals of this kind will have been a basic part of the life of the agricultural communities of Canaan long before Israel came to be established there.

It is also the case that in the Old Testament itself the associations with the saving events of the people's past are not thoroughly integrated into the text until a very late stage. Passover and Unleavened Bread are described (e.g. in Exod. 12) in a way which makes it highly probable that these are basically separate observances, only subsequently brought together. The linkage of the feast of Weeks with Sinai is only developed in post-biblical texts, and the explanation that Tabernacles originated in the 'booths' (an alternative translation of the Hebrew word) of greenery found in the wilderness (Lev. 23: 43) at once strikes us as implausible; the whole point of a wilderness is the absence of such booths of greenery.

It is this autumn festival, of Booths or Tabernacles, that has been the subject of much scholarly speculation in recent years. It seems clear that in the pre-exile period it was the chief of the annual festivals, and only from the exile on did Passover become the main observance. The role of the king in the autumn festival has been much discussed, for one of the themes of that festival was that it was almost certainly the beginning of a New Year, with concerns for continuing prosperity and fertility in the coming year. As we have already seen, the king was pictured as the channel through which God's grace flowed to his people, and therefore it is almost certain that he will have played some important role in the festival. The Psalms celebrating the king's role may find their origin in such an observance.

Significant also is the fact that the vine harvest will have been completed, and there are numerous texts which hint at the joy with which this was commemorated (Judg. 21 is a well-known example). Almost certainly one of the developments in the religious awareness of Israel will have been an increasing puritan strand, a feeling that Israel's God was not to be worshipped in rites that might readily degenerate into sexual excess; the warnings in the Deuteronomistic literature against 'whoring' after other gods make excellent sense in such a context.

Both the book of Deuteronomy and prophets such as Jeremiah can be seen as those who are claiming that the worship of Yahweh should be different from the religious practice of their neighbours; and it would appear as if they, and others who thought in similar terms, were successful in attributing the blame for the destruction of Jerusalem and the exile to the depravity which they claimed had polluted the true worship of Israel's God. Historically they may not have been justified; in terms of giving a coherent explanation of the course of events they were strikingly successful.

Something of the same kind can be seen with the development of sacrificial worship. Previous to the exile this had characteristically been a joyful occasion, carried out in the context of the extended family. In the later period, however, the stress came overwhelmingly to be on sacrifice as a means of atonement for sin, and this feature runs throughout the descriptions of the sacrificial rites in Leviticus 1–7. However diverse their origin, all are here brought together as means of ensuring that sin did not retain its hold on the community or on its individual members.

The God of Israel

This brings us to our third area of concern: religious belief. By the end of the Old Testament period the Jews were known for the firmness with which they held to the belief in only one God. The *shema'* begins with Deuteronomy 6: 4, translated in RSV as 'Hear, O Israel: the LORD our God is one LORD'. But uncertainty as to the precise nuances of this summons is well illustrated by the fact that the margin offers three different ways of translating the four Hebrew words which make up its latter part. It is clearly a call to the faithful Israelite to limit his devotion to Yahweh alone; it is less clear that it is an assertion of the existence of only one God. In any case, as we have already seen, much of Deuteronomy is better understood as a plea for what should be done rather than an objective statement of what is actually common practice.

The plain fact is that the origins of the worship of Yahweh are extremely obscure, and right down to the time of the exile two quite different types of approach as to the nature of this worship can be found among reputable scholars and supported by plausible evidence.

One view is that the worship of Yahweh was from the outset significantly different from that addressed to other gods by other, neighbouring peoples. Such an understanding may be linked with the view that Yahweh was a god of history, or a god who moved with his people, as against other gods whose primary associations were with the agricultural round or who were to be worshipped in one place. On this view the religious history of the period down to the exile is very largely a matter of constant falling away from true worship, both at the popular level and also through official syncretism: the building of a state temple in Jerusalem would have been a concession to worship of a different type, and the rejection of a temple as an appropriate place for the worship of Yahweh in 2 Samuel 7 would have been an expression of this 'higher' Yahwism. The great prophets of the monarchical period—Samuel, Elijah, Amos, Hosea, Isaiah—could then be seen as those who recalled the kings and the people back to known standards of the past from which they had fallen away, either through ignorance or through deliberate wickedness or folly.

Such a view is widely held, and has the advantage that it is not far distant from the internal presentation found in the Old Testament itself. Even at the most superficial level, however, it can be seen that so neat a picture contains inconsistencies. For example, we have already noted that the festivals in honour of Yahweh were essentially agricultural festivals, celebrating the annual round of harvest. The holy places at which he was worshipped, and the cultic personnel involved in that worship, were essentially similar, as we have also seen, to those of the surrounding peoples. There is, furthermore, an inherent difficulty in supposing the continued

separate existence of a group of people in the middle of the
Israelites carrying on a separate cult which could be described as
'Canaanite', and which acted as a source of temptation to the
devotees of Yahweh.

The difficulty of accepting the biblical account as essentially
preserving accurate historical information has been increased by
recent archaeological finds, such as those at Tell Arad, in the south
of Judah. (As far as is known, the only biblical reference to the site is
the brief allusion at Judg. 1: 16.) Excavations here have shown that
through the greater part of the monarchical period there existed a
temple, which must have been quite independent of the 'royal'
temple at Jerusalem, and appears to have been unaffected by the
drive toward centralization of worship under Josiah.

Again, as we have already noted, among an extensive collection of
ostraca (potsherds) discovered at another site in Judah, Kuntillet
Ajrud, there are references to 'Yahweh and his Asherah'. Asherah
was a Canaanite goddess, symbolized by a wooden pole associated
in some way with fertility, and one would never suppose from the
text of the Old Testament that her worship could be associated
with, or countenanced alongside, that of Yahweh himself. Taken
together with some of the evidence from proper names it may well
be that the distinctive character of the demands and worship of
Yahweh only came to be widely propagated in the last centuries
before the exile, by what has sometimes been described as the
'prophetic minority'. If this were so, it would probably be legitimate
to see how the destruction of Jerusalem and the exile was
interpreted not only as a political disaster, which it undoubtedly
was, but also as a religious opportunity: a chance for those
committed to the worship of Yahweh alone, as utterly different from
all other so-called gods, to impose their views on the community,
bewildered by the break-up of so much of the traditional pattern of
their lives. If this is so, we can properly speak of the imposition of a
distinctive theology as the norm for the community's future
existence; and it is to the theological understanding of the material
that we must turn for our final chapter.

Is a Theology Possible?

We have given much attention in this book to changes and developments that have affected biblical study in recent years. It might be supposed that after so much upheaval it would be possible to turn to theology as an unchanging still centre amidst all the turmoil. Such an expectation would soon be rudely shattered; theological thinking has undergone dramatic changes, not least when the question has arisen of the kind of theology which can legitimately be derived from the biblical text.

What is an Old Testament theology?

In the 1950s and 1960s several theologies of the Old Testament were written; they characteristically focused upon some particular theme which the author regarded as able to give a coherent and unifying structure to the whole body of material. There was also an influential viewpoint known as the 'biblical theology' movement, which attempted to draw together elements from both Old and New Testaments so as to make a coherent theology which would result in one presentation able to embrace the whole Christian Bible, again by using some over-arching theme, such as the 'acts of God', as a structure to make a unity out of material which seemed at first sight very varied.

Neither of these approaches is now widely adopted. The hidden assumptions which underlay them have been challenged, and those theologies of the Old Testament which have been written in recent years have concentrated as much on methodology—what should such a volume contain and how should it be organized?—as on presenting a theology according to already agreed norms. In such a situation it is inevitable that our proposals in this section must be of a tentative nature, but it still remains true that there are significant points of a theological character that can legitimately be raised.

In the remainder of this chapter four theological issues will be touched upon, which seem to serve the essential double function of arising directly from the Old Testament text itself and of having something to say to the present-day reader of that text. (It is easy enough to see that if either of these preconditions is lacking, the legitimacy or value of the whole exercise will soon be called into question.) The four points may be briefly stated, before being spelt out in somewhat greater detail in what follows. They are:

- (a) The affirmations of the Old Testament about God and his nature, which set out more explicitly what is often taken for granted in the New Testament and later tradition;
- (b) The concern of the Old Testament for community as against merely individual values in its ordering of the world;
- (c) The critique offered in the prophets and elsewhere of a nominally religious society;
- (d) The acceptance of a radical scepticism within the tradition, prepared to challenge received beliefs, yet remaining acceptable to those who handed down that tradition to their successors.

All of these points are clearly theological, in the sense that they arise directly from the nature of the Old Testament belief in God; all of them are equally of significance for a religious understanding of our contemporary situation.

What kind of a God?

It is commonly held, even among those predisposed to be sympathetic to the biblical tradition, that the God of the Old Testament is harsh and vindictive, in sharp contrast to the God of love presented in the New Testament. To some extent it is possible to rebut this kind of comment in two ways: by drawing attention to the actual statements found in the Old Testament setting out the character of Israel's God; and by underlining the fact that the God worshipped by Jesus and his followers in the New Testament is the same God as we learn of from the Old Testament. The second of these points is marginal to the concerns of this book, and cannot be pursued further here; but the first demands further consideration.

It is noteworthy that several times in the Old Testament there are statements of a kind analogous to a creed, setting out the character of Israel's God. Thus in Exodus 34: 6 f. we have: 'The LORD, a God merciful and gracious, slow to anger and abounding in steadfast love and faithfulness, keeping steadfast love for thousands, forgiving iniquity and transgression and sin, but who will by no means clear the guilty'. Individual elements of this confession are found elsewhere in the Old Testament (e.g. Num. 14: 18; Jer. 32: 18; Joel 2: 13; Nahum 1: 3; and frequently in the Psalms). The variety of these contexts shows that this understanding was not confined to any one tradition within the Old Testament, and the usage of the Psalms suggests that it found its most natural expression in the context of worship. That does not imply that it should be regarded as merely a series of intellectual assertions about the character of God, as the recital of creeds in Christian worship has sometimes been understood; an important element in this confession is the way it stresses the *personal* qualities of God.

This matter of personhood is an issue to which we shall need to return, but for the moment we should note that many of the characteristics postulated of God are precisely those which are demanded by the prophets and others as the best expressions of true human behaviour. The word in the Exodus passage translated as 'steadfast love' is the Hebrew word *ḥesed*, and the prophets emphasize that this is required also of human behaviour; in the well-known passage in Hosea 6: 6, God is presented as saying 'I desire steadfast love and not sacrifice' as the appropriate form of behaviour among his worshippers. There is to be, that is to say, an analogy between the way in which the divine character is perceived and the demands made on human beings; and it is in the eighth-century prophets that we first find this kind of analogy accepted as a basis for their message. God is not unpredictable, liable to forms of behaviour which bring his worshippers to despair; the best of human behaviour can in some way be seen as reflecting the divine character.

And yet the unease remains: there undoubtedly are many places in the Old Testament where God's behaviour *is* presented as vindictive, tyrannical, unpredictable; where it almost seems as if God is the villain of the piece. No theological presentation can be legitimate which fails to take due notice of material of this kind.

We should note first of all that it is important to distinguish statements of this kind from those where God's punishment of the wicked is postulated. In the Exodus passage already quoted the last assertion made was that God would by no means clear the guilty. Much modern religious thought finds it difficult to come to terms with this idea of divine punishment, but if God is to be spoken of as 'judge' (or even 'king' or 'father'; and all of these are regular biblical metaphors used of God), it is difficult to see how the idea of the need for punishment can be totally excluded.

The next comment which can legitimately be made in this context is that the descriptions of divine capriciousness are human descriptions, that is to say, they reflect the viewpoint of their authors. The Bible may sometimes be referred to as 'the Word of God', but that can surely not mean that divine utterances are received by us or by the original authors in some direct way, which guarantees precise verbal accuracy. What we have is a record of human perceptions of divine words and actions, and human perceptions in all ages are fallible. In particular, religious believers are always liable to suppose that God is on their side and therefore opposed to their enemies; and it is but one step from that point to a conviction that God can legitimately be presented as hating and being prepared to destroy such enemies.

This can happen both at the national and at the individual level. In Exodus 17: 8–16 we have an account of a battle between Israelites and Amalekites which ends with Israel's victory, and the attribution to Yahweh of the intention 'utterly to blot out the remembrance of Amalek from under heaven'; and this enmity between Israel and Amalek is recalled in 1 Samuel 15, where the gruesome tale ends with the statement that 'Samuel hewed Agag [the Amalekite king] in pieces *before the LORD* in Gilgal'. Many accounts of battles in Joshua and Judges start from the same presupposition: that Israel is the people of Yahweh, Yahweh is Israel's God, and that their interests are therefore tightly bound together, and that in national crisis total warfare must meet with divine approval.

What is true at the national level is equally applicable for the individual. Those Psalms sometimes known as 'cursing Psalms' display an exactly similar mentality. Psalm 109 is a case in point, where in verses 6–19 every kind of misery and misfortune is invoked against the psalmist's enemies. Again the underlying assumption is that the psalmist himself is a loyal servant of God; that this implies that anyone opposed to him must automatically be opposed to God; and that God's vengeance can legitimately be invoked against such opponents. We are not invited to share, or to approve, such sentiments; but we shall do well to remember that in the last years of the twentieth century they are as widespread as ever: religious fanatics of every kind remain totally certain that their cause is also God's cause and that God's support can be invoked with complete confidence. (We shall note a significantly different approach within the Old Testament at pp. 156 f. below.)

One commonly proposed way of easing this problem of perceptions of God which seem dangerously inadequate is to describe them as 'primitive', an early stage in human development. There may be value in such an approach, but it needs to be adopted with care. We have just noted how widespread even today are religious feelings and expressions remarkably similar to those we find offensive in the Old Testament, so it would be quite misleading to suppose that humanity has in some way sloughed off these 'primitive' characteristics in its upward march to higher perceptions of God. Again there is the very obvious danger of a circular argument: there are virtually no objective criteria available for deciding which texts are 'early'. Often they are assigned early dates simply because of the supposedly 'primitive' features which they display.

Despite these reservations there do appear to be some valuable insights to be gained from this idea of development. As we saw in the last chapter, it is very probable that Israel's perception of God underwent a significant change at around the time of the exile, when the community experienced a series of disasters which transformed both its self-perception and its understanding of God and the divine workings. A less national, and more universal, mode of understanding seems to have become widespread from this period. Prophetic writings such as Isaiah 40–55 or Jonah are often cited as illustrating this development, but we may take just two other examples. First, this is the most probable date of composition of the great Priestly account of creation in Genesis 1, which makes clear how all created existence is part of the divine order, and that God's care can in no way be limited to Israel. Secondly, the book of Job, though it probably takes as its framework an ancient folk-tale, is likely to have reached its final form in this period, and it shows clearly how the assumptions about God's enemies being the same as human enemies are totally misplaced.

From this period comes also the insistence on the oneness of God, typified by the *shema'* (Deut. 6: 4). It is disputed whether or not it is appropriate to use the Greek term 'monotheism' in the Old Testament, for that implies a philosophical conviction that there can only be one God. The Old Testament is more practically based; instead of speculation how many gods there might be, it asserts that Yahweh is the only effective God; other gods are ineffective, worse than useless, objects fit only for mockery. This is a theme found frequently in Isaiah 40–5. Such an attitude can have its unattractive features, especially as we live in days when we are rightly warned of the offensive aspects of the mockery of the religious beliefs of others; it is also important to see how great an advance on most earlier belief about God it represented.

The Israel of the post-exilic era was, of course, as liable as religious communities of both earlier and later ages to fall short of perceptions of this kind in times of crisis; but at least those perceptions were clearly present in the traditions being handed down in the community.

Two final points, closely related to each other, may be made about the Old Testament presentation of God and his activity. Though, as we have seen, there are a few places in which this is presented in quasi-credal form, the most characteristic mode of describing God and his dealings with humanity is by means of stories, in which God is regularly pictured as one of the participants. This is especially marked in the Pentateuch, where God's conversations with Abraham or Moses present him as if he were at one level to be understood as one of those involved in the drama; it soon becomes clear on careful reading that there is a good deal more to be said about God than that! This kind of presentation is, however, not confined to the 'historical' texts; in the account of prophetic calls, for example, God is again found as engaging in direct conversation with Isaiah or Jeremiah or Amos.

To those used to a more formal and abstract way of speaking of God, whether through the creeds of the Christian Church, or through the speculations of philosophers, all this can be highly disconcerting. Yet, as we saw in an earlier chapter, much modern study is taking a particular interest in the literary character of the Old Testament, in which stories play an important part. It is not difficult to see that story is indeed a highly effective and very usual way of conveying one's understanding of a human being, and so it is not surprising to discover that an analogous way of envisaging God and his actions came to be so important. This indeed is part of what is meant by describing God as 'personal' rather than in any abstract way. At times we may feel that this personal mode of reference is carried rather far, as in the way in which the Old Testament often speaks of God becoming angry or changing his mind, but these are modes of human speech which may be regarded as the inevitable concomitants of using it to speak about God. To obtain a balanced picture it is important also to bear in mind those frequent passages which describe God in the language of worship and mystery; his holiness, his otherness, is something of which human beings must stand in awe.

This leads on to the second concluding point which needs to be made in our sketch of the Old Testament portrayal of God. If we are to feel that we have adequate knowledge and understanding of any other person, we must be able to discern some consistency in his or her behaviour and characteristics; we must, as the expression goes, 'know where we are' with that person. Much of the Old Testament can be seen as a probing toward just such an understanding of God. That God's hand could be seen, even in such unlikely events as the destruction of Jerusalem and its temple, and the exile of its leading citizens, that a consistent pattern could be discerned and traced in the events that had befallen both the community at large and individuals within it: such a perception not only made sense of human experience, it also helped to provide a consistent and credible picture of the God whom his worshippers believed to be controlling affairs, by reminding them that the power of God was to be seen in disaster as much as in prosperity.

A community concern

Religion has been presented by some modern writers as if it were a purely individual matter; such an understanding is quite alien to what we find in the Old Testament. There are laws and prophetic oracles which appear to be addressed to individuals, but overwhelmingly the concern is with the community. And that concern is not limited simply to religious practice; the sets of values which are laid down are primarily applicable to the community as a whole.

A key word for the understanding of the Old Testament is the word 'covenant'; indeed, a more accurate translation than 'Testament' for both parts of the Bible would be 'Old and New Covenants'. There has been much discussion among scholars whether this was an ancient term, perhaps borrowed by the Israelites from its use by other nations when they made treaties laying down their future relations with one another. In fact, as far as our evidence goes, it only became widespread at around the time of the exile: it is common in Jeremiah (esp. chs. 31–4) and Ezekiel (e.g. chs. 16f.), but rare in earlier prophetic writings, and is also frequently used by the writers of Deuteronomy and of the Priestly material in the Pentateuch. It came indeed to be a basic means of describing the nature of the relation between God and his community, and as such the idea was projected back so that Noah, Abraham, and Moses were all pictured as recipients of a divine covenant on behalf of the community (Gen. 9, 15, 17; Exod. 24). The relation between God and the Davidic king was also understood as a covenant (e.g. Ps. 89); in that way of understanding the divine dealings with his people the picture was of the king as the channel through whom the blessings of the covenant were to be conveyed.

This covenant status was essentially a community matter. It was not something into which individuals entered. Even the apparent exceptions to this—the patriarchs and the king—do not really change the picture, for they are covenant recipients in virtue of their representative status *vis-à-vis* the community.

It is in this context that the prophetic condemnations are most appropriately understood, whether or not the word 'covenant' is actually used in a particular prophetic collection. It remains a matter of uncertainty to whom, or in what circumstances, these prophetic words were addressed, but it is clear that they were not aimed at individuals; the whole community was the subject of condemnation. This might affect what we would now call social abuses—the failure to grant their rights to the poor, the dishonest practices engaged in by traders and those in business. But it is perhaps even more striking to find religious practice as the subject of fierce attacks. What should be the way in which a society can most properly approach its God has instead become the supreme example of the way in which that society has come to be corrupted.

Amos provides vivid illustrations of this point. In chapters 2 and 6 in particular we find severe attacks upon sharp practice in the market-place, but most striking of all is the way in which he condemns the lavish religious ceremonies of the community (5: 18 ff.); this most obvious way of keeping in God's favour is in fact compounding their offence. (This, though not a 'story' about God in the sense mentioned in the previous section, has the same effect; of allowing us to see that for Amos, like the other prophets, God was a being whose interests and concerns were by no means confined to religious matters. One wonders if that misapprehension about God which they condemn is entirely extinct even today.)

This interplay between the individual and the larger society is characteristic of all parts of the Old Testament. It has sometimes been overstated, as if ancient Israel knew nothing of the individual, but regarded corporate identity as supreme. One should beware of those scholarly theories, still sometimes found, which speak of the prophets of the exile, Jeremiah or Ezekiel, as the 'discoverers of the individual'; there are many passages in every part of the Old Testament which make it clear that awareness of individuals, of their needs and responsibilities, was as great in the society of ancient Israel as in any other.

And yet the fact remains that the Old Testament writings illustrate a greater sense of group solidarity than we are nowadays accustomed to. The genealogies make it clear that an important part of a person's identity arose from the clan or extended family of which she or (more usually) he was a member. Many of the laws have as their underlying assumption the fact of interdependence between one member of society and another; this is shown not only by humanitarian concerns like those expressed in the laws in Deuteronomy (chs. 24 and elsewhere) that alien immigrants, orphans, and widows are not neglected or treated harshly, but also in the mundane but extremely important requirements for community living found in the laws in Exodus 21–2. Comparable demands are of course found throughout the prophetic books.

The Old Testament insists throughout on the interdependence of different strata of society: rich upon poor and poor upon rich, young upon old and old upon young. Here is an important theological truth often neglected in the modern West, and one of the lessons from the Old Testament which liberation theology, to which we referred in an earlier chapter, may be able to teach those who are willing to listen.

Condemnation of religious practice

We saw in the last section how condemnation of current religious practice occasioned the violent denunciations of Amos. He was of course not alone in this; as we have noted in earlier chapters, all the eighth-century prophetic collections have similar attacks upon the religious practice of the time: Isaiah 1: 10–17; Hosea 6: 6; Micah 6: 6–8 are among the best-known such passages, but they are by no means isolated in their context. The tradition was maintained by Jeremiah (ch. 7 and elsewhere), though in later prophetic collections it has given way to a different stress, upon the importance of true worship to the community seeking to re-establish itself once again in Jerusalem after the disruptions caused by enemy invasions.

How should these condemnations be understood? An older view, still occasionally found, is to take them at their apparent face value and to suppose that they imply a complete rejection of formal worship. Only when freed from the shackles of cultic requirements could the community be free to worship its God in a fitting manner.

Such an understanding appears, however, to be seriously anachronistic. As we saw in the last chapter, religious practice throughout the ancient world meant cult, and the prophets were men of their time, even if they had attained to a deeper understanding of its requirements than most of their contemporaries. It is most unlikely, therefore, that the prophets envisaged the possibility of the abandonment of religious practice, and there are indeed other passages in their books which regard it as axiomatic. Rather, we should understand their condemnations in a different way: they saw the superficiality of much that was done in the name of worship as symptomatic of a deeper malaise. Their fellow-countrymen by and large had no real recognition of what commitment to Yahweh implied. Religious practice was indeed essential; it was being systematically debased.

Put simply (perhaps over-simply) the point can be made thus. The prophets saw in their fellow-countrymen an enthusiastic commitment to the worship of the national God, but this commitment had no recognition of what was really required if such worship was to be acceptable. The point can be illustrated from the wonderfully ironic passage in Micah 6: 6–8, where the prophet pictures his hearers as supposing that God's favour can be won by the sheer extravagance of their worship ('thousands of rams . . . ten thousands of rivers of oil') or by dramatic gestures which would force a divine response ('Shall I give my first-born for my transgression?'). The prophet makes it clear that what God really requires, and always has done, is something less dramatic but much more demanding: 'to do justice, to love kindness (*ḥesed*), and to walk humbly with your God'. It is often held that this passage is a later addition to the words of the original prophet Micah, but whatever its origin it is of primary importance for its insistence that acceptable religious practice must be based on more than the show of outward observance.

This passage, though apparently addressed to individuals ('O man'), is in reality a demand made upon the whole community in its ordering of worship. This draws our attention to an important difference between the Old and New Testaments. The New Testament writings are for the most part addressed to those who have become committed members of a new and enthusiastic group set in the midst of larger communities whose religious and social practices were very different from their own. There was no prospect of anything like a 'national Christianity' in the first century AD or for a long time afterwards.

The Old Testament situation is quite different. Though our knowledge of who precisely its different writings were originally addressed to is extremely fragmentary, it is clear that as they were handed down the Old Testament writings address the tension between a national religion, of which all members of the state are regarded as adherents, and the religion of a minority community making its primary appeal to the committed. There is a striking similarity here at some levels with the situation in Britain and other modern Western countries. They are sometimes described as Christian countries, yet it is clear that in any meaningful form Christianity is a minority commitment, of whose demands the great majority of the population would be largely ignorant. Yet any suggestion put to such people that they were not Christian would be met with great indignation. Perhaps Israel and Judah at some periods of their history were 'Yahwistic countries' in the same sense that Britain is a 'Christian country'. If there is any force in the analogy one might gain new insights from reading the prophetic books in particular.

A place for doubt

Reference to committed minorities and the like might give the impression that the Old Testament is essentially concerned only with those who are prepared to accept a particular religious viewpoint, to set aside any doubts they might have, to engage whole-heartedly in the worship of the one just and powerful God, Yahweh. It might appear in short as if the Old Testament was a collection of religious polemic of a kind still familiar today, even if expressed somewhat differently.

Up to a point this may be true. There is little indication of atheism in ancient Israel. One Psalm, repeated twice in the Psalter in slightly varying forms, does indeed begin 'The fool says in his heart, "There is no God"' (Pss. 14: 1; 53: 1), but this seems to be a kind of practical atheism implying that there are those whose conduct makes no allowance for the fact that they are under God's surveillance, rather than any kind of intellectual rejection of God's existence. To that extent, therefore, the Old Testament is a book for believers.

But not all the believers share the untroubled confidence in the power and justice of God which religious propaganda characteristically sets out. In those poems in the book of Jeremiah which are sometimes known as his 'confessions' (found between chs. 11 and 20 in the present form of the book) God is pictured as completely misleading his faithful servant (Jer. 20: 7f.). In the book of Job the pious hero is the victim of a bet in Heaven of which by definition he can know nothing, which leads to all his family and possessions being taken from him in a series of disasters, and in the poems which follow he goes on to speak in the harshest terms of the impossibility of obtaining any justice from God. The book Ecclesiastes is framed by a kind of motto, which recurs throughout and shapes its whole approach: 'Vanity of vanities, all is vanity' (Eccles. 1: 2; 12: 8). For this author, too, there is no way in which much that goes on in his world can be explained. Similar expressions can be found in some Psalms and scattered elsewhere in the Old Testament. If the Old Testament gives no indication of doubts as to God's existence there are clear enough pointers to the fact that there were those who were puzzled or sceptical as to the evidence for his justice in ordering human affairs.

Perhaps the most remarkable point to be made here is that these doubts are found within the pages of the Old Testament itself. These are not the expressions of some heretical group at odds with the ruling authorities; those who handed the tradition down have felt able to include these questionings within that body of revered writings. There will be those today who find such deviations from the wisdom of the received tradition disturbing and anomalous; for others the fact that a religious tradition is prepared to allow such doubts and questionings is one of the causes which make it worthy of our attention in the twentieth century.

BIBLIOGRAPHY

Since this volume is envisaged as introductory to the series, there is much in the other volumes of the series which develops in greater detail the material discussed here.

A helpful discussion of a wide range of recent developments in Old Testament study can be found in D. A. Knight and G. M. Tucker (eds.), *The Hebrew Bible and its Modern Interpreters* (Scholars Press, 1985).

Chapter 1
ROGERSON, J. W. (ed.), *Beginning Old Testament Study* (SPCK, 1983).

Chapter 2
BARR, J., *Comparative Philology and the Text of the Old Testament* (OUP, 1968; repr. Eisenbraun, 1987).
KLEIN, R. W., *Textual Criticism of the Old Testament* (Fortress Press, 1974).
VERMES, G., *The Dead Sea Scrolls: Qumran in Perspective* (SCM Press, 2nd edn., 1982).
WÜRTHWEIN, E., *The Text of the Old Testament* (Eerdmans/SCM Press, 1979).

Chapter 3
There are numerous volumes devoted to the history of ancient Israel, but many of them are little more than a retelling of the biblical account. Among those that recognize the problems that this involves may be mentioned:
HAYES, J. H., and MILLER, J. M. (eds.), *Israelite & Judaean History* (SCM Press, 1977).
SOGGIN, J. A., *A History of Israel* (SCM Press, 1984).

Among other books dealing with the issues raised in this chapter may be noted:
COOTE, R. B., and WHITELAM, K. W., *The Emergence of Early Israel in Historical Perspective* (Almond Press, 1987).

MILLER, J. M., *The Old Testament and the Historian* (Fortress Press, 1976).

RAMSEY, G. W., *The Quest for the Historical Israel* (John Knox Press, 1981/SCM Press, 1982).

THOMPSON, T. L., *The Historicity of the Patriarchal Narratives* (de Gruyter, 1974).

Chapter 4

LANCE, H. D., *The Old Testament and the Archaeologist* (Fortress Press, 1981/SPCK, 1983).

MOOREY, P. R. S., *Excavation in Palestine* (Lutterworth Press, 1981).

THOMAS, D. W. (ed.), *Archaeology and Old Testament Study* (OUP, 1967).

WISEMAN, D. J., *Chronicles of Chaldaean Kings* (British Museum, 1956).

Chapter 5

CARROLL, R. P., *When Prophecy Failed* (SCM Press, 1979).

GOTTWALD, N. K., *The Tribes of Yahweh* (SCM Press, 1979).

LEMCHE, N. P., *Ancient Israel* (JSOT Press, 1988).

RODD, C. S., 'On Applying a Sociological Theory to Biblical Studies', *JSOT* 19 (1981), 95–106.

WILSON, R. R., *Prophecy and Society in Ancient Israel* (Fortress Press, 1980).

—— *Sociological Approaches to the Old Testament* (Fortress Press, 1984).

Chapter 6

DOUGLAS, M., *Purity and Danger* (Routledge, 1969).

KIRKPATRICK, P. G., *The Old Testament and Folklore Study* (JSOT Press, 1988).

LANG, B., *Anthropological Approaches to the Old Testament* (Fortress Press/SPCK, 1985).

LEACH, E., and AYCOCK, D. A., *Structuralist Interpretations of Biblical Myth* (CUP, 1983).

ROGERSON, J. W., *Anthropology and the Old Testament* (Blackwell, 1978; repr. JSOT Press, 1984).

Chapter 7

BERRYMAN, P., *Liberation Theology* (Tauris, 1987).

COGGINS, R. J., 'The Contribution of Women's Studies to Old Testament Studies: A Male Reaction', *Theology* (1988), 5–16.

GOTTWALD, N. K., *The Bible and Liberation* (Orbis, 1984).
RUETHER, R. R., *Sexism and God-Talk* (SCM Press, 1983).
TRIBLE, P., *Texts of Terror* (Fortress Press, 1984).

Chapter 8
ALTER, R., and KERMODE, F. (eds.), *The Literary Guide to the Bible* (Collins, 1987).
BARTON, J., *Reading the Old Testament: Method in Biblical Study* (DLT, 1984).
JACOBSON, D., *The Story of the Stories* (Secker & Warburg, 1982).
ROBERTSON, D., *The Old Testament and the Literary Critic* (Fortress Press, 1977).

Chapter 9
The subject-matter of this chapter figures prominently in a very large amount of literature devoted to the Old Testament, and therefore to make a selection is even more difficult than usual. The first two books are older standard works dealing with the history of Israel's religion and the religious institutions; the remaining items reflect some of the challenges to older views characteristic of more recent scholarship.

DE VAUX, R., *Ancient Israel* (DLT, 1961).
RINGGREN, H., *Israelite Religion* (SPCK, 1966).

BARKER, M., *The Older Testament* (SPCK, 1987).
LANG, B., *Monotheism and the Prophetic Minority* (Almond Press, 1983).
NICHOLSON, E. W., *God and his People* (OUP, 1986).

Chapter 10
CLEMENTS, R. E., *Old Testament Theology* (Marshall Morgan & Scott, 1978).
DAVIDSON, R., *The Courage to Doubt* (SCM Press, 1983).

INDEX OF PASSAGES CITED

In certain passages, especially in the Psalms, the Hebrew verse numbers are slightly different from those in the English versions. The English chapter and verse classification is cited here, and the books are listed in the order of the English Versions.

Old Testament

GENERAL INDEX